THE YEAR YOU WERE BORN

1971

A fascinating book about the year 1971 with information on:
Events of the year UK, Adverts of 1971, Cost of living, Births, Deaths, Sporting events,
Book publications, Movies, Music, World events and People in power.

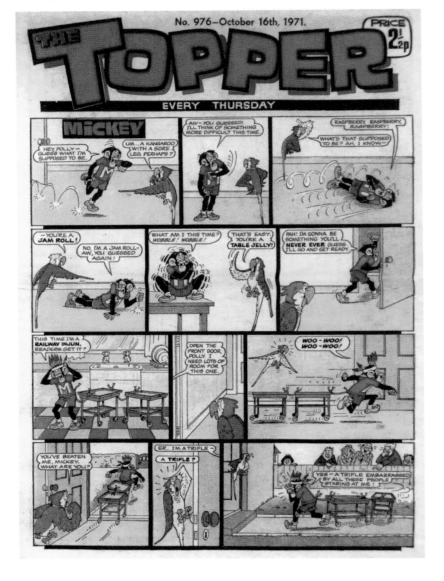

INDEX

Page 3   **Events of the year UK**

Page 15   **Adverts in 1971**

Page 22   **Cost of living**

Page 24   **Births**

Page 30   **Deaths**

Page 31   **Sporting events**

Page 39   **Book Publications**

Page 42   **Movies**

Page 53   **Music**

Page 61   **World Events**

Page 77   **People in power**

UK EVENTS OF 1971

January

1st The Divorce Reform Act 1969 came into effect, allowing couples to divorce after a separation of two years (five if only one of them agrees). A divorce can also be granted on the grounds that the marriage has irretrievably broken down, and it is not essential for either partner to prove "fault". It is revealed on the 19th January 1972 that the number of divorces in Britain during 1971 exceeded 100,000 for the first time.

2nd The Ibrox Disaster: The disaster occurred on the 2nd January 1971, when 66 people were killed in a crush as supporters tried to leave the stadium. The match was an Old Firm game (Rangers v Celtic) and was attended by more than 80,000 fans. In the 90th minute, Celtic took a 1–0 lead through Jimmy Johnstone and some Rangers supporters started to leave the stadium. However, in the final moments of the match, Colin Stein scored an equaliser for Rangers. As thousands of spectators were leaving the ground by stairway 13, it appears that someone may have fallen, causing a massive chain-reaction pile-up of people. The loss included many children, five of them schoolmates from the town of Markinch in Fife. The youngest child to die was Nigel Patrick Pickup of Liverpool, age 9. Most of the deaths were caused by compressive asphyxia, with bodies being stacked up to six feet deep in the area. More than 200 other fans were injured.

3rd BBC Open University broadcasts began.

8th Tupamaros kidnapped Geoffrey Jackson, British ambassador to Uruguay, in Montevideo; they kept him captive until September.

12th The Hertfordshire house of Robert Carr, Secretary of State for Employment, was bombed. Nobody was injured.

14th "The Angry Brigade", an extremist group, admitted responsibility for the bombing of Robert Carr's house, as well as planting a bomb at the Department of Employment offices at Westminster.

The Commonwealth Heads of Government Meeting 1971 was the first Meeting of the Heads of Government of the Commonwealth of Nations (formerly named the British Commonwealth). It was held in Singapore, between the 14th January 1971 and the 22nd January 1971, and was hosted by that country's Prime Minister, Lee Kuan Yew. British prime minister Edward Heath advised Queen Elizabeth II not to attend the conference due to a row within the Commonwealth over Britain selling arms to South Africa. It would be the only CHOGM the Queen would miss until 2013. Ugandan president Milton Obote was overthrown by Idi Amin in a military coup, whilst he was attending the meeting. At the meeting the Singapore Declaration of Commonwealth Principles was agreed setting out the core political values that would form the main part of the Commonwealth's membership criteria.

20th The first ever postal workers' strike took place, led by UPW General Secretary Tom Jackson, in an attempt to win a 19.5% pay rise.

21st After collapsing in March 1969 a newly reconstructed Emley Moor transmitter in West Yorkshire starts again. Now a concrete tower, at 1084 feet (330.4m), it is Britain's tallest freestanding structure.

February

1st | The Broadcast receiver licence was abolished for radios.

3rd | Tyneside-set British crime film Get Carter starring Michael Caine premièred (in Los Angeles).

4th | Rolls Royce go bankrupt: In the new year of 1971 financial problems caused largely by development of thi new RB211 turbofan engine designed and developed for Lockheed Aircraft Corporation's new L-1011 TriStar led, after several government-provided cash subsidies, to the recognition Rolls-Royce had no resources left and it voluntarily entered receivership the 4th February 1971. There were said to have been acrimonious telephone conversations between US president Richard Nixon and the British prime minister Edward Heath but these were subsequently denied. Responding to questions as to how the situation coul have arisen, the chief executive advised that in their calculations they were guided by the success of their estimates in the launching of their Spey engine. Had the government simply nationalised Rolls-Royce it would have been unable to avoid the obligations to Lockheed. The situation was handled in the usual manner with the assets being sold for cash, in this case to the government, leaving the massive liabilities to be dealt with by Rolls-Royce Limited using the funds realised by the sale. However the government would not fix a purchase price for the assets until the situation became clearer because without a continuing business many of them might be worthless. In the meantime the government would use the assets to continue the activities of the aero-engine, marine and industrial gas turbine and small engine divisions that were important to national defence, the collective programmes with other countries and to many air forces and civil airlines. A new company (1971) was incorporated that May to purchase substantially the whole of the undertakings and assets of the four divisions of Rolls-Royce connected with gas turbine engines. The original company, Rolls-Royce Limited, was placed in liquidation on the 4th October 1971.

11th | The UK, along with the USA, the USSR and others signed the Seabed Treaty, outlawing nuclear weapons o the ocean floor.

15th | Decimalisation: Decimal Day: the U.K. and the Republic of Ireland both switched to decimal currency. Decimal Day in the United Kingdom and in Ireland was on the 15th February 1971, the day on which each country decimalised its respective £sd currency of pounds, shillings, and pence. Before this date, in the United Kingdom, the British pound was made up of 20 shillings, each of which was made up of 12 pence, total of 240 pence. With the decimalisation, the pound kept its old value and name, and the only changes were in relation to the subunits. The shilling was abolished, and the pound was subdivided into 100 "new pence" (abbreviated "p"), each of which was worth 2.4 "old pence" (abbreviated "d"). In Ireland, the Irish pound had a similar £sd currency structure and similar changes took place.

February

5th Enoch Powell predicted an "explosion" unless there was a massive repatriation scheme for the immigrants.

24th Home Secretary Reginald Maudling announced the Immigration Bill that is set to strip Commonwealth immigrants of their right to remain in the United Kingdom. The bill is supported by Enoch Powell, but the former shadow cabinet minister continued to demand a massive voluntary repatriation scheme for the immigrants.

March

1st An estimated 120,000 to 250,000 "kill the bill" protesters went on strike against the 1971 Industrial Relations Act in London. The Industrial Relations Act 1971 was an Act of the Parliament of the United Kingdom, since repealed. It was based on proposals outlined in the governing Conservative Party's manifesto for the 1970 general election. The goal was to stabilize industrial relations by forcing concentration of bargaining power and responsibility in the formal union leadership, using the courts. The act was intensely opposed by unions, and helped undermine the government of Edward Heath. It was repealed in 1974 when the Labour Party returned to government.

7th Following the recent protests in London, some 10,000 striking workers protested in Glasgow against the Industrial Relations Bill.

8th The Postal workers' strike ended after 47 days.

10th The 1971 Scottish soldiers' killings took place in Northern Ireland during The Troubles. It happened on the 10th March 1971, when the Provisional Irish Republican Army shot dead three unarmed British Army soldiers of the 1st Battalion, Royal Highland Fusiliers. Two of the three soldiers were teenage brothers; all three were from Scotland. They were murdered off-duty and in civilian clothes, having been lured from a city-centre bar in Belfast, driven to a remote location and shot whilst relieving themselves by the roadside. Three British soldiers had been killed prior to this event; all had been on duty and killed during rioting. The deaths led to public mourning and protests against the Provisional IRA. Pressure to act precipitated a political crisis for the government of Northern Ireland, which led to the resignation of Northern Ireland Prime Minister James Chichester-Clark. The British Army raised the minimum age needed to serve in Northern Ireland to 18 in response to this incident. In 2010 a memorial was dedicated to the three soldiers near to where they were killed in north Belfast.

20th Maj. James Chichester-Clark resigns as Prime Minister of Northern Ireland. He is succeeded on the 23rd March by Brian Faulkner.

April

1st The United Kingdom lifted all restrictions on gold ownership. Since 1966 Britons were banned from holding more than four gold coins or from buying any new ones, unless they held a licence.

11th Ten British Army soldiers were injured in rioting in Derry, Northern Ireland.

15th The planned Barbican Centre was given the go-ahead.

April

18th The station opened on the 1st April 1867 as "Kentish Town", was renamed "Kentish Town West" on the 2nd June 1924, and closed after a serious fire on the 18th April 1971. Despite an announcement in 1976 that the station would not reopen, it was rebuilt and re-opened on the 5th October 1981 under British Rail.

19th Unemployment reached a post-Second World War high of nearly 815,000.

27th Eight members of the Welsh Language Society went on trial for destroying English language road signs in Wales.

British Leyland launched the Morris Marina which succeeded the Minor (a smaller model, production of which ceased after 23 years with 1.6 million sold) and Oxford models and was similar in size to the Ford Cortina (to which it had been designed as a direct competitor), Vauxhall Victor and Hillman Hunter. It has 1.3 and 1.8 litre petrol engines, rear-wheel drive and a choice of four-door family saloon and two-door coupé body styles, with a five-door estate set to follow in the next two years.

May

1st A bomb planted by the Angry Brigade exploded in the Biba Kensington store. Biba was a London fashion store of the 1960s and 1970s. Biba was started and primarily run by the Polish-born Barbara Hulanicki with help of her husband Stephen Fitz-Simon.

2nd The Daily Mail was relaunched as a tabloid.

6th Singer Dickie Valentine is killed in a car accident on the Glangrwyney bridge near Crickhowell.

8th Arsenal won the FA Cup final with a 2–1 win over Liverpool at Wembley Stadium. Substitute Eddie Kelly became the first substitute to score in an FA Cup final and it was only the second time this century (and the fourth time ever) that an English team has completed the double of the Football League First Division and the FA Cup.

May

11th The Daily Sketch, Britain's oldest tabloid newspaper was withdrawn from circulation after 62 years. The Daily Sketch was a British national tabloid newspaper, founded in Manchester in 1909 by Sir Edward Hulton. The Daily Sketch was a British national tabloid newspaper, founded in Manchester in 1909 by Sir Edward Hulton. It was bought in 1920 by Lord Rothermere's Daily Mirror Newspapers, but in 1925 Rothermere sold it to William and Gomer Berry (later Viscount Camrose and Viscount Kemsley).It was owned by a subsidiary of the Berrys' Allied Newspapers from 1928 (renamed Kemsley Newspapers in 1937 when Camrose withdrew to concentrate his efforts on The Daily Telegraph). In 1946, it was merged with the Daily Graphic. In 1952, Kemsley decided to sell the paper to Associated Newspapers, the owner of the Daily Mail, who promptly revived the Daily Sketch name in 1953. The paper struggled through the 1950s and 1960s, never managing to compete successfully with the Daily Mirror, and in 1971 it was closed and merged with the Daily Mail.

20th Chelsea F.C., last year's FA Cup winners, won the European Cup Winners' Cup with a 2–1 win over Real Madrid of Spain in Athens, Greece.

23rd "The Unknown Bairn": The drowned body of a young boy is found washed up onshore at Tayport; he is never identified.

25th Production begins at the Invergordon aluminium works.

28th Opening of the Llanberis Lake Railway. The Llanberis Lake Railway is a 1 ft 11 1/2 in (597 mm) narrow gauge heritage railway that runs for 2.5 miles (4 km) along the northern shore of Llyn Padarn in north Wales in the Snowdonia National Park. The starting point is the town of Llanberis at the eastern end of the lake, with the western terminus at Pen Llyn in the Padarn Country Park. The return journey takes around 60 minutes.

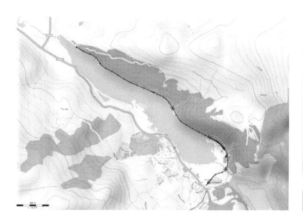  

June

7th The children's show Blue Peter buried a time capsule in the grounds of BBC Television Centre, due to be opened on the first episode of the year 2000.

14th The first Hard Rock Cafe opened near Hyde Park Corner in London.

Education Secretary Margaret Thatcher's proposals to end free school milk for children aged over seven years were backed by a majority of 33 MPs.

June

15th Several Labour run councils threatened to increase rates in order to continue the free supply of milk to school children aged over seven years, in reaction to Thatcher's plans to end free milk supply to school children of that age group. Thatcher defends her plans, saying that the change will free more money to be spent on the construction of new school buildings.

Upper Clyde Shipbuilders entered liquidation.

20th Britain announced that Soviet space scientist Anatoli Fedoseyev had been granted asylum.

21st Britain began new negotiations for EEC membership in Luxembourg.

24th The EEC agreed terms for Britain's proposed membership and it was hoped that the nation will join the EEC next year.

25th The first Reading Festival "of jazz and progressive music" took place. The Reading Festival is the world's oldest popular music festival still in existence. Many of the UK's most successful rock and pop bands have played at the festival, including The Rolling Stones, Fleetwood Mac, The Kinks, Pink Floyd, Deep Purple, The Who, Cream, Black Sabbath, Judas Priest, Genesis, Thin Lizzy, Iron Maiden, The Jam, The Police, Status Quo, The Pogues, Blur, Pulp, Muse, The Cure, Radiohead, The Libertines, Arctic Monkeys, Biffy Clyro and Oasis. The festival has also hosted prominent international acts such as Alice Cooper, Twisted Sister, The Doobie Brothers, Iggy Pop, AC/DC, Metallica, Mika, Slipknot, Guns n' Roses, Eminem, Nirvana, Hole, Foo Fighters, blink-182, The Strokes, Green Day, Faith No More, My Chemical Romance, and Red Hot Chili Peppers.

The festival has had various musical phases over the years, but since the current two-site format was adopted in 1999, rock, alternative, indie, punk and metal have been the main genres featured in the line-up. More recently hip hop has comprised an increasing proportion of the line-up, including headline sets by artists such as Kendrick Lamar and Post Malone.

July

1st	The film Sunday Bloody Sunday is released, one of the first mainstream British films with a bisexual theme. The film is significant for its time in that Finch's homosexual character is depicted as successful and relatively well-adjusted, and not particularly upset by his sexuality. In this sense, Sunday Bloody Sunday was a considerable departure from Schlesinger's previous film Midnight Cowboy (1969), which portrayed its queer characters as alienated and self-loathing, as well as other gay-themed films of the era, including The Boys in the Band (1970) and Some of My Best Friends Are... (1971)
2nd	Royal Scots Dragoon Guards formed as the senior Scottish regiment of the British Army at Holyrood, Edinburgh, by amalgamation of the Royal Scots Greys and 3rd Carabiniers.
6th	Police launched a murder investigation after three French tourists are found shot dead in Cheshire.
8th	Two rioters were shot dead by British troops in Derry, Northern Ireland.
13th	Barlaston man Michael Bassett, 24, was found dead in his fume-filled car. Police identified him as their prime suspect in the recent triple French tourist murder in Cheshire.
14th	The Criminal Damage Act abolished the – theoretically capital – offence of arson in royal dockyards.
16th	The Social Democratic and Labour Party (SDLP) announces that it is withdrawing from the Parliament of Northern Ireland.
23rd	The final section of London Underground's Victoria line, from Victoria to Brixton, was opened by Princess Alexandra.

29th	The United Kingdom opted out of the Space Race, with the cancellation of its Black Arrow launch vehicle.
30th	Upper Clyde Shipbuilders workers began to take control of the shipyards in a work-in under the leadership of Jimmy Reid.

August

1st | It becomes legal to register marriages in the Welsh language.

6th | Chay Blyth became the first person to sail around the world east to west against the prevailing winds. Chay Blyth became the first person to sail non-stop westwards around the world, aboard the yacht British Steel taking 292 days, and as a result was made a Commander of the Order of the British Empire (CBE).

9th | British security forces in Northern Ireland detained hundreds of guerrilla suspects and put them into Long Kesh prison - the beginning of an internment without trial policy. Twenty died in the riots that followed, including eleven in Ballymurphy Massacre. The Ballymurphy Massacre was a series of incidents between the 9th and 11th August 1971, in which the 1st Battalion, Parachute Regiment of the British Army killed eleven civilians in Ballymurphy, Belfast, Northern Ireland, as part of Operation Demetrius. The shootings were later referred to as Belfast's Bloody Sunday, a reference to the killing of civilians by the same battalion in Derry a few months later.

Internment without trial is introduced in Northern Ireland. In Operation Demetrius, over 300 republicans are 'lifted' in pre-dawn raids. Some loyalists are later arrested.

11th | Prime Minister Edward Heath participated in the British victory in the Admiral's Cup yacht race.

12th | British troops begin clearing operations in Belfast following the worst rioting in years. Taoiseach Jack Lynch calls for an end to the Stormont administration.

14th | The Who released their critically acclaimed album Who's Next.

15th | Showjumper Harvey Smith was stripped of his victory in the British Show Jumping Derby by judges for making a V sign. His career was often controversial; in 1971 he was disciplined (overturned on appeal) after he gave a "V sign" to the judges following a near perfect round which won him the British Show Jumping Derby for the second year in succession and also a 'tongue-in-cheek' part in an advert for Victory V sweets with the slogan 'They've got a kick like a mule!' Smith became so famous that he embarked on a brief, but unsuccessful, singing career. His sons, Robert and Steven, also became equestrian champions.

21st | Kyle of Tongue Bridge and causeway opened, replacing a ferry.

1st	The pre-decimal penny and threepence ceased to be legal tender.
3rd	Qatar gained independence from the United Kingdom. Unlike most nearby emirates, it declined to become part of either the United Arab Emirates or Saudi Arabia.
7th	The death toll in The Troubles of Northern Ireland reached 100 after three years with the death of 14-year-old Annette McGavigan, who was fatally wounded by a gunshot in crossfire between British soldiers and the IRA.
9th	British Ambassador Geoffrey Jackson was freed after being held captive for eight months by extreme left-wing guerrillas in Uruguay. Geoffrey Jackson was kidnapped by Tupamaros guerrillas on 8 January 1971 in Montevideo, Uruguay. He was released after eight months of captivity, on 9 September 1971. Three decades later it became known that Edward Heath, the British prime minister at that time, negotiated a deal for Jackson's release. £42,000 was paid for his release, which was brokered by Salvador Allende, the Chilean president who enjoyed contacts with the Tupamaros rebels.
16th	Stirling and Falkirk by-election: Labour retains the seat but the Scottish National Party takes second place with a surge of 20% in their support.
21st	The television music show The Old Grey Whistle Test was aired for the first time on BBC 2. It was commissioned by David Attenborough and aired on BBC2 from 1971 to 1988. It took over the BBC2 late night slot from Disco 2, which ran between September 1970 and July 1971, while continuing to feature non-chart music.
	The show was devised by BBC producer Rowan Ayers. The original producer, involved in an executive capacity throughout the show's entire history, was Michael Appleton. According to presenter Bob Harris, the programme derived its name from a Tin Pan Alley phrase from years before. When they got the first pressing of a record they would play it to people they called the old greys – doormen in grey suits. Any song they could remember and whistle, having heard it just once or twice, had passed the old grey whistle test.

24th	Britain expelled 90 Russian diplomats for spying, following revelations made by a KGB defector; fifteen are not allowed to return.

October

1st | Godfrey Hounsfield's invention, the CAT scan, was used for the first time on a patient at a hospital in Wimbledon. A CT scan or computed tomography scan (formerly computerized axial tomography scan or CAT scan) makes use of computer-processed combinations of many X-ray measurements taken from different angles to produce cross-sectional (tomographic) images (virtual "slices") of specific areas of a scanned object, allowing the user to see inside the object without cutting. The 1979 Nobel Prize in Physiology or Medicine was awarded jointly to Allan M. Cormack and Godfrey N. Hounsfield "for the development of computer assisted tomography."

CT History

- First test images in 1967
- First clinical images ~ 1971
- First commercial scanner 1972

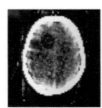

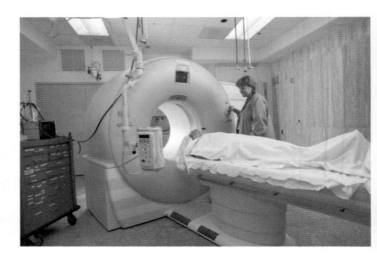

13th | The British Army began destroying roads between the Republic of Ireland and Northern Ireland as a security measure.

21st | A gas explosion in the town centre of Clarkston, East Renfrewshire killed twenty people.

The television drama Edna, the Inebriate Woman is shown on BBC One. The play deals with an elderly woman, Edna (Patricia Hayes), who wanders through life in an alcoholic haze without a home, a job or any money. A rambling, pathetic yet defiant woman, Edna sleeps rough and begs for food and shelter and the drama follows her progress as she moves from hostel to hostel, going to a psychiatric ward and then prison along the way. At the end, a small home for homeless women run by Josie Quinn (Barbara Jefford) from a Christian charity, 'Jesus Saves', is closed down after an inquiry, following the complaints of neighbours. Edna and the other women are on the road again.

23rd | Two women were shot dead by soldiers in Belfast as their car failed to stop at a checkpoint.

28th | The United Kingdom became the sixth nation successfully to launch a satellite into orbit using its own launch vehicle, the Prospero (X-3) experimental communications satellite (built at the Royal Aircraft Establishment, Farnborough), using a Black Arrow carrier rocket from Woomera Launch Area 5 in South Australia.

30th | The Democratic Unionist Party was founded by the Rev. Ian Paisley in Northern Ireland.

31st | A bomb, probably planted by the Angry Brigade, exploded at the top of the Post Office Tower in London.

November

1st | Erin Pizzey establishes the world's first domestic violence shelter in Chiswick, London.

10th | The 10-route Spaghetti Junction motorway interchange was opened north of Birmingham city centre, incorporating the A38 (M) (Aston Expressway) and the southern section of the M6 motorway. The interchange would have a total of 12 routes when the final stretch of the M6 was opened the following year.

22nd | The Cairngorm Plateau disaster occurred on the 22nd November 1971 when six fifteen-year-old Edinburgh school students and their two leaders were on a navigational expedition in a remote area of the Scottish mountains. When the weather deteriorated they adopted their emergency plan and headed for the Curran shelter, but they failed to reach it and became stranded for two nights on the high plateau in a blizzard. Five children and the leader's assistant died of exposure. A sixth student and the group's leader survived the ordeal with severe hypothermia and frostbite. The tragedy, also often called the Feith Buidhe disaster, is regarded as Britain's worst mountaineering accident.

December

2nd | On the 4th December 1971, the Ulster Volunteer Force (UVF), an Ulster loyalist paramilitary group, detonated a bomb at McGurk's Bar in Belfast, Northern Ireland. The pub was frequented by Irish Catholics/nationalists. The explosion caused the building to collapse, killing fifteen Catholic civilians — including two children — and wounding seventeen more. It was the deadliest attack in Belfast during the Troubles. Despite evidence to the contrary, the British security forces asserted that a bomb had exploded prematurely while being handled by Irish Republican Army (IRA) members inside the pub, implying that the victims themselves were partly to blame. A report later found that the police were biased in favour of this view, and that this hindered their investigation. The victims' relatives allege that the security forces deliberately spread disinformation to discredit the IRA. In 1977, UVF member Robert Campbell was sentenced to life imprisonment for his part in the bombing and served fifteen years. The bombing sparked a series of tit-for-tat bombings and shootings by loyalists and republicans, which contributed to making 1972 the bloodiest year of the conflict.

December

3rd	The Queen's yearly allowance was increased from £475,000 to £980,000.
10th	Dennis Gabor won the Nobel Prize in Physics "for his invention and development of the holographic method".
16th	Banking and Financial Dealings Act passed, updating the definition of bank holidays in the U.K.
29th	The United Kingdom gave up its military bases in Malta.
30th	The seventh James Bond film – Diamonds Are Forever – was released. Sean Connery, who appeared in the first five films before being succeeded by George Lazenby for On Her Majesty's Secret Service in 1969, returned to the role for one final appearance.

Sir Thomas Farmer: One of seven siblings in a devoutly Catholic family, in 1964 Farmer founded his own tyre retailing business which he sold in 1969 for £450,000. Thomas Farmer retired to the United States, but became bored and decided to find a new challenge. He returned to Edinburgh to found the Kwik Fit chain of garages in December 1971. The firm grew quickly, mainly through acquisition, including opening in the Netherlands in 1975. Farmer was named Scottish Businessman of the Year in 1989. After building the chain to become the world's largest independent tyre and automotive repair specialists with over 2,000 centres operating in 18 different countries, Farmer sold the firm to Ford in 1999 for more than £1 billion. He is the first Scot to be awarded the prestigious Andrew Carnegie Medal for philanthropy.

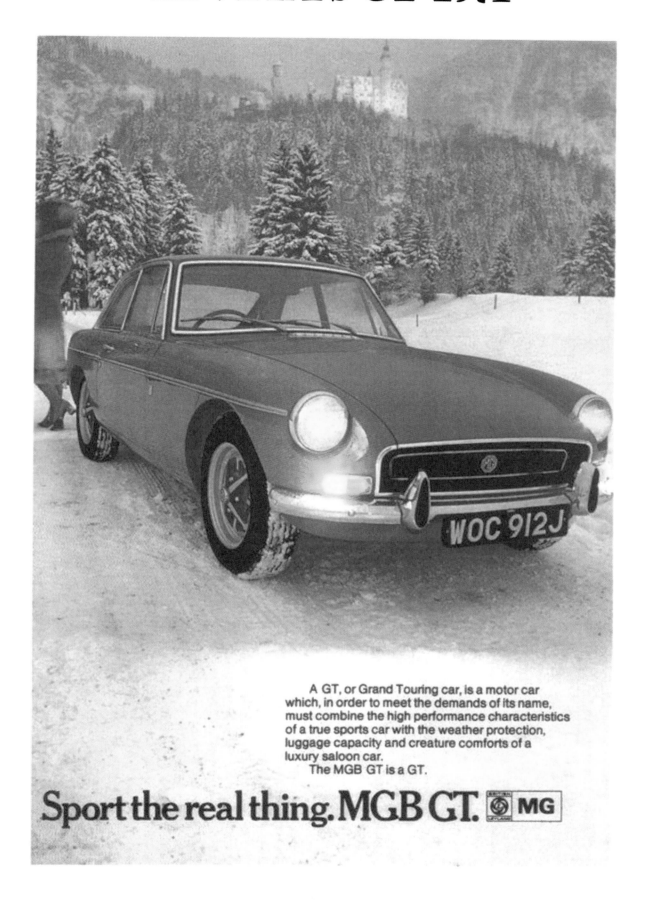

A GT, or Grand Touring car, is a motor car which, in order to meet the demands of its name, must combine the high performance characteristics of a true sports car with the weather protection, luggage capacity and creature comforts of a luxury saloon car.
The MGB GT is a GT.

Sport the real thing. MGB GT. MG

3·3 litre big seater Cresta.

Two's company – three's a crowd. Whoever said that hadn't heard about Cresta. Because Cresta is made for big people and a lot of them.

Even five big people can be very much at their ease in Cresta's five seat luxury.

Luxury like rich, deep upholstery, full carpeting and optional fully reclining front seats. And five big people can get where they want to go, fast and comfortably.

Cresta's 6 cylinder, OHV, 140 bhp engine gets them there fast.

Cresta's light, positive steering, tenacious road-holding, and choice of manual or GM automatic transmission gets them there effortlessly. De luxuriously in fact.

3.3 litre big seater Cresta – for the big people in life. Cresta de luxe £1,534.

Also available Cresta £1,416. Prices ex-factory including pt.

7

We brought it back from Mexico.

We spent two years building an Escort for the London to Mexico Rally and, after it had cleaned up down there, it suddenly occurred to us: wouldn't it be a shame not to offer this kind of car to everybody?

Yes, we decided it would.

Gentlemen, the Escort Mexico– except for a more economical power plant and a few other nice little improvements, the same car that beat the world. 1600GT engine uprated to 86 bhp (din) at 5,500 rpm, close ratio gearbox, stiffened and lowered suspension, specially strengthened body, servo assisted brakes, 5½J wheels with radials, uprated half shafts, radius arms, stone-deflector plates–the whole shooting match.

All of which will wind up to a hundred. And hit sixty in less than eleven seconds.

How much does a rally winner cost? You'd expect it to cost a bomb. (That's what it cost us.) But we're only asking £1,150.

So, if you've always regretted missing out on the world's toughest rally, cheer up. At least now you can own the car that won it!

The Escort Mexico. The road version of the rally winner.

RECOMMENDED RETAIL PRICE IS £1,150.4.0. PRICE INCLUDES PURCHASE TAX AND DELIVERY TO FORD DEALERS IN THE UK (EXCLUDING N. IRELAND) ACCORDING TO STATUTORY REGULATIONS FRONT INERTIA REEL SEAT BELTS ARE FITTED. THESE ARE SUPPLIED AT EXTRA COST

A Sprinter in a Saville Row suit
THE FIAT 125

What more can be said?

Fiat 125 Saloon—Inclusive 12 months road tax, delivery charges ex-works, number plates and seat belts, £1304.12.0.
Fiat 125 Special—Inclusive 12 months road tax, delivery charges ex-works, number plates and seat belts, £1454.14.9.

Ask these people

BRAND (MOTOR) ENGINEERS LTD.
RINGSFIELD ROAD, BECCLES. Tel. 2224

CLUERS CARS
SOUTH DENES ROAD, GT. YARMOUTH. Tel. 4042

GRAHAM GERRISH & COMPANY
EAGLE GARAGE, NEWMARKET ROAD, NORWICH. Tel. 25927

HILL AND OSBORNE LTD.
ST. GERMANS, KING'S LYNN. Tel. St. Germans 296

HILL & OSBORNE (NORFOLK) LTD.
BURNHAM MARKET, Nr. FAKENHAM. Tel. Burnham Mkt. 234

PRETTY BROS.
DISS ROAD, SCOLE, NORFOLK. Tel. Scole 628

WATT BROS.
NORWICH ROAD, AYLSHAM. Tel. Aylsham 2134

WAVENEY GARAGES
WAVENEY DRIVE, LOWESTOFT. Tel. 2014

WOODLAND CAR SALES LTD.
SALHOUSE ROAD, NORWICH. Tel. Norwich 34285

THE POINTER MOTOR COMPANY
AYLSHAM ROAD, NORWICH. Tel. Norwich 45345 (4 lines)
A Mecca Group Company

Beccles

Great Yarmouth

Norwich

St. Germans

Burnham Market

Scole

Aylsham

Lowestoft

Norwich

DISTRIBUTORS for
NORFOLK and SUFFOLK

They will drive you into raptures

Manta. Wild and beautiful for five.

New formula from Opel Why should bachelors have all the fun? The new Opel Manta is here. And it's the one car in the world guaranteed to change your ideas on family motoring.

The Manta formula means sports car performance, saloon car comfort Wild and beautiful for five—it looks like pure power. But inside, there's room for your wife and family in superb comfort. Put your foot down and you're in touch with more power than you ever dreamed of. Yet the Manta has enough safety features to fill the most timid with confidence. The Manta has a 1.6 litre engine. It develops a cool 92 bhp, a maximum speed of 102 mph, and acceleration to match. Takes off with a grace that will leave

sports car fanatics green with envy. And all the while it cushions you and yours in the soft luxury of contoured seats. Lets them look at the world through deep wrap-around windows. Gives them brilliantly engineered suspension. A dual-circuit braking system, discs on the front. And really family-size luggage space in the boot.

Choose the new one from Opel. Manta. Wild and beautiful for five. At your Opel dealer now!

MANTA

General Motors Limited, Vehicle Division, Stag Lane, London NW9.

"It's a new Opel"

VALIANT 3p
AND TV21

EVERY MONDAY   4TH DECEMBER, 1971

WHO IS IT?

THIS REMARKABLE BRITISH PILOT LOST BOTH HIS LEGS AFTER A FLYING ACCIDENT IN 1931. BUT FITTED WITH ARTIFICIAL LIMBS HE RETURNED TO THE R.A.F. AND FOUGHT WITH DISTINCTION IN THE BATTLE OF BRITAIN IN 1940...

HE WAS SHOT DOWN OVER FRANCE IN 1941 AND REMAINED IN A GERMAN P.O.W. CAMP UNTIL AFTER THE WAR, WHEN HE LED THE VICTORY FLY-PAST OVER LONDON IN SEPTEMBER 1945...

THIS COURAGEOUS MAN HAS PROVED BY EXAMPLE THAT A PERSON WITH ARTIFICIAL LEGS CAN LEAD A FULL AND ACTIVE LIFE. TODAY HE IS A TOP EXECUTIVE WITH AN OIL COMPANY. HE CAN DANCE, DRIVE, AND PLAYS GOLF.

You'll find the answer on IT'S ALL YOURS page inside!

Malaysia 50 cents   Malta 10d   Australia 12 cents   East Africa 1/25   West Africa 1/2d   South Africa 12 cents   Rhodesia 13 cents   New Zealand 12 cents

THE BEANO

The Comic With "MINNIE the MINX"!

No. 1514—July 24th, 1971.   EVERY THURSDAY 2p

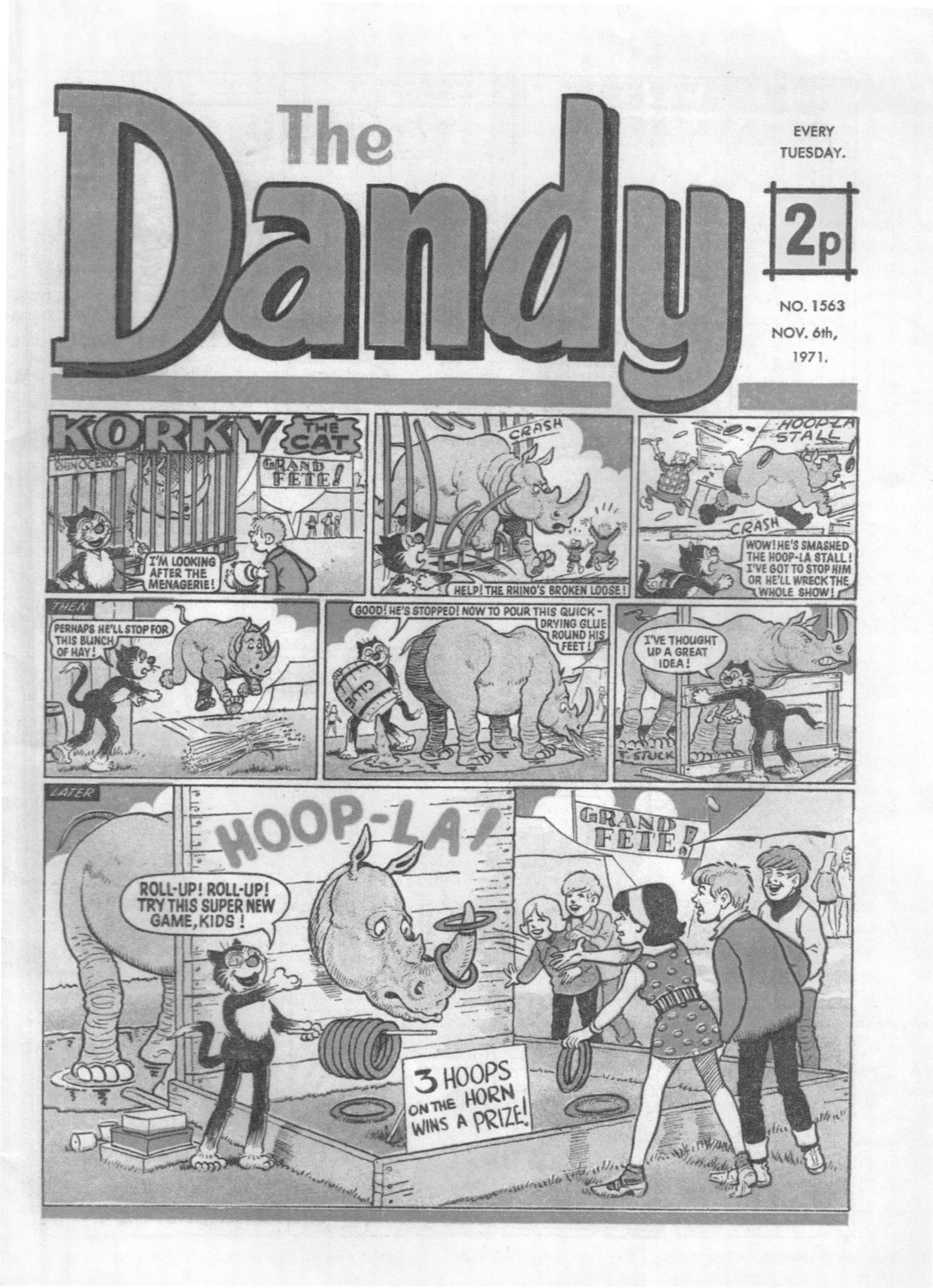
The Dandy
EVERY TUESDAY.
2p
NO. 1563
NOV. 6th, 1971.
KORKY THE CAT
RHINOCEROS
GRAND FETE!
I'M LOOKING AFTER THE MENAGERIE!
CRASH
HELP! THE RHINO'S BROKEN LOOSE!
HOOP-LA STALL
CRASH
WOW! HE'S SMASHED THE HOOP-LA STALL! I'VE GOT TO STOP HIM OR HE'LL WRECK THE WHOLE SHOW!
THEN
PERHAPS HE'LL STOP FOR THIS BUNCH OF HAY!
GOOD! HE'S STOPPED! NOW TO POUR THIS QUICK-DRYING GLUE ROUND HIS FEET!
GLUE
I'VE THOUGHT UP A GREAT IDEA!
STUCK
LATER
HOOP-LA!
GRAND FETE!
ROLL-UP! ROLL-UP! TRY THIS SUPER NEW GAME, KIDS!
3 HOOPS ON THE HORN WINS A PRIZE!

Stereo in your car
with Philips car cassette players

PHILIPS

21

COST OF LIVING 1971

A conversion of pre-decimal to decimal money

The Pound, 1971 became the year of decimalization when the pound became 100 new pennies. Prior to that the pound was equivalent to 20 shillings. Money prior to 1971 was written £/s/d. (d being for pence). Below is a chart explaining the monetary value of each coin before and after 1971.

Symbol	Before 1971	After 1971
£	Pound (240 pennies)	Pound (100 new pennies)
s	Shilling (12 pennies)	5 pence
d	Penny	¼ of a penny
¼d	Farthing	1 penny
½d	Halfpenny	½ pence
3d	Threepence	About 1/80 of a pound
4d	Groat (four pennies)	
6d	Sixpence (Tanner)	2½ new pence
2s	Florin (2 shillings)	10 pence
2s/6d	Half a crown (2 shillings and 6 pence)	12½ pence
5s	Crown	25 pence
10s	10 shilling note (10 bob)	50 pence
10s/6d	½ Guinea	52½ pence
21s	1 Guinea	105 pence

Prices are in equivalent to new pence today and on average throughout the UK.

Item	1971	Price equivalent today
Wages, average yearly	£1,202.00	£16,832.00
Average house price	£4,741.00	£66,374.00
Price of an average car	£1,160.00	£16,240.00
Litre of petrol	£0.08p	£1.05p
Flour 1.5kg	£0.12p	£1.68p
Bread (loaf)	£0.09p	£1.26p
Sugar 1kg	£0.09p	£1.26p
Milk 1 pint	£0.20p	£2.80p
Butter 250g	£0.12p	£1.67p
Cheese 400g	£0.20p	£2.86p
Potatoes 2.5kg	£0.10p	£1.40p
Bacon 400g	£0.34p	£4.82p
Beer (Pint)	£0.17p	£1.64p

The UK and Irish Governments' decision to decimalise the currency, switching from 240 to 100 pennies in a pound or punt, presented a big problem for shops. Every cash register had to be converted, and every assistant who operated the tills had to be retrained.

Most retailers decided to dual price items for a period of time, showing both the old and the new values, meaning that every sign in-store had to be changed twice and on-product labels also had to be replaced.

The move hit Woolworth particularly hard, as it paid the price for resisting the introduction of self-service. As a result it had four times as many tills to convert as it would have done if it had already moved to central cash desks or checkouts. Converting them took every penny of available investment and thousands of hours of staff training.

For more than five hundred years Great Britain's currency was based around twelves rather than tens. The 'duo-decimal' currency consisted of pounds, shillings and pence. There were twelve pennies (abbreviated to "D" for denarii, the Latin name for penny) in a shilling, and twenty shillings in a pound, meaning that there were 240 old pennies in a pound.

BRITISH BIRTHS

Alan McManus was born on the 21st January 1971and from Glasgow, Scotland. H is a professional snooker player and snooker commentator. Alan McManus has long been considered a consistently good player, having a record of fourteen consecutive seasons in the Top 16, but never managed to achieve the success of his contemporaries Stephen Hendry, Ken Doherty, Ronnie O'Sullivan, John Higgins, Mark Williams, Matthew Stevens and Paul Hunter. He was ranked in the Top 16 from 1990 to 2006, dropping out after an unsuccessful 2005/2006 season He lost a World Championship qualifier 9–10 to journeyman Joe Delaney in 2007 McManus started the 2017/2018 season at number 32 in the world rankings; an would reach the third round of both the 2017 China Championship and 2017 Pau Hunter Classic. He would also reach the second round of the 2017 UK Championship with a 6–3 win over Robin Hull; before losing a final frame decide to Jimmy Robertson 5–6.

Gail Porter was born on the 23rd March 1971 and grew up in Edinburgh, Scotland. She is a Scottish television presenter, television personality, former model and actress. After making an unsuccessful bid to join the presentation team of the BBC children's show Blue Peter. She has presented family-friendly television programmes, or ones aimed at children. They include Children's BBC Scotland, T.I.G.S, MegaMag, Up For It!, Children in Need, Fully Booked, The Movie Chart Show, Top of the Pops, and Live & Kicking, work for CITV, and The Big Breakfast. In 2005 Porter developed alopecia totalis, losing her hair. She decided not to wear a hat or wig in order to raise awareness of the condition. She is a vice-president of The Children's Trust, a UK charity for children with brain injuries. In 2017 she became the brand ambassador for the insolvency practitioner Creditfix, meeting with the public and speaking openly about her struggles with debt in several corporate videos. Gail is also a black belt in karate.

David Marshall Coulthard, MBE was born on the 27th March 1971, known as DC and is a Scottish former Formula One racing driver turned presenter, commentator and journalist. David Coulthard began karting at the age of eleven and achieved early success before progressing to car racing in the British Formul Ford Championship and the Formula 3000 series. He first drove in Formula One with Williams in the 1994 season succeeding the late Ayrton Senna. The followir year he won his first Grand Prix in Portugal, and then for the 1996 season he moved to McLaren. After winning two races in the 1997 season, he finished 3rd the World Drivers' Championship in the 1998 season. After retiring from Formul One Coulthard continued working with Red Bull as a consultant and joined the BBC as a commentator and pundit for their coverage of Formula One. David Coulthard has also participated in the Race of Champions, finishing runner-up in the Drivers' Cup in 2008, and winning the competition in 2014 and 2018. Since 2016 he has worked as a commentator and analyst for Channel 4 after they took over the BBC's terrestrial television rights.

Ewan Gordon McGregor OBE was born on the 31st March 1971 and is a Scottish actor known internationally for his various film roles, including independent dramas, science-fiction epics, and musicals. Six months prior to his graduation from Guildhall, McGregor won a leading role in Dennis Potter's six-part Channel 4 series Lipstick on Your Collar (1993). Not long afterwards, he starred in the BBC adaptation of Scarlet and Black (also 1993) with a young Rachel Weisz, and made his film debut in Bill Forsyth's Being Human (1994). He was cast as the young Obi-Wan Kenobi in Star Wars: Episode I – The Phantom Menace (1999); the character was originally played by Sir Alec Guinness in the first Star Wars trilogy. A motorcyclist since his youth, McGregor undertook a marathon international motorbike trip with his best friend Charley Boorman and cameraman Claudio von Planta in 2004. From mid-April to the end of July, they travelled from London to New York via central Europe, Ukraine, Kazakhstan, Mongolia, Russia, Canada and the United States on BMW R1150GS Adventure motorbikes.

Karen Dunbar was born on the 1st April 1971 and is a Scottish comedian, actress and writer. Born in Ayr and raised in Glasgow. Karen Dunbar rose to prominence when she appeared in the BBC Scotland comedy series Chewin' the Fat (1999-2002) and was subsequently given her own show by the channel, the Karen Dunbar Show (2003-2006). Dunbar began her career as a DJ and karaoke host before she attended The Comedy Unit's open auditions in 1997 where she was cast in the BBC Scotland comedy sketch show Chewin' the Fat. She was subsequently given her own show by the channel, The Karen Dunbar Show, which received two coveted Golden Rose nominations for Best Comedy Show and Karen herself two personal nominations for Best Comedy Performance. In October 2017 Dunbar appeared in BBC Scotland's River City for a special one-off appearance. She played the part of Francesca Simpson, estranged wife of Pete Galloway. In 2019, Dunbar appeared in the tours Calendar Girls and Still Game Live: The Final Farewell.

Charles Cumming was born on the 5th April 1971 is a British writer of spy fiction. Cumming was born in Ayr in Scotland and educated at Ludgrove School (1979–1984), Eton College (1985–1989) and the University of Edinburgh (1990–1994), where he graduated with 1st Class Honours in English Literature. Charles Cumming's first novel, A Spy by Nature was published in the UK in June 2001. The novel's hero, Alec Milius, is a flawed loner in his early 20s who is instructed by MI5 to sell doctored research data on oil exploration in the Caspian Sea to the Central Intelligence Agency. In August 2001, Cumming moved to Madrid. His second novel, The Hidden Man (2003), tells the story of two brothers investigating the murder of their father, a former SIS officer, at the hands of the Russian mafia. The Hidden Man also examines the clandestine role played by SIS and the CIA during the Soviet–Afghan War.

Charles has written 9 novels so far.

David John Tennant was born on the 18th April 1971 and is a Scottish actor. At the age of three, Tennant told his parents that he wanted to become an actor because he was a fan of Doctor Who, but they tried to encourage him to aim f more conventional work. Tennant was awarded his first major TV role as the manic depressive Campbell in the BBC Scotland drama series Takin' Over the Asylum (1994). Doctor Who returned to British screens in March 2005, with Christopher Eccleston playing the role of the Ninth Doctor in the first series. Tennant replaced him as of the second series, making his first, brief appearanc as the Tenth Doctor in the episode "The Parting of the Ways". In October 2015 Big Finish Productions announced that Tennant would return to the role of the Tenth Doctor alongside Catherine Tate as his former companion Donna Noble three new stories from Big Finish. In November 2017, three new audio dramas were released by Big Finish Productions with Tennant once again starring as th Tenth Doctor, alongside Billie Piper as Rose Tyler.

Craig MacLean MBE was born on the 31st July 1971 and is a Scottish track cyclist who has represented Great Britain and Northern Ireland at the 2000 Summer Olympics in Sydney and the 2004 Summer Olympics in Athens, winning a Silver Medal in the Team Sprint at the 2000 Olympics. Born in Grantown-on-Spey, MacLean kicked off his cycling career as second man in the Great Britain Team Sprint until switching to lead man in 2002. He broke the GB kilometre record at the Olympic Trials in 2004. MacLean's career as a member of the British elite team came to a close in 2008. He suffered from a mystery illness (later diagnosed as Coeliac disease) for the majority of his career so could no longer perform at the level required. As a sighted guide, McLean returned to the sport in its Paralympic form, piloting Neil Fachie to two gold medals in the 2011 UCI Para-cycling Track World Championships, and Anthony Kappes to a gold medal in the 2012 Paralympic Games.

He was appointed Member of the Order of the British Empire (MBE) in the 2013 New Year Honours for services to cycling.

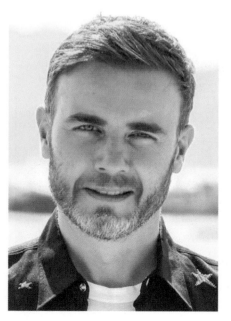

Gary Barlow OBE was born on the 20th January 1971 and is an English singer, songwriter, pianist, record producer, actor and film score producer. In 1986, when Barlow was 15 years old, he entered a BBC Pebble Mill at One Christma song competition with "Let's Pray for Christmas". After reaching the semi-finals, he was invited to London's West Heath Studios to record his song. This inspired him to perform on the northern club circuit, singing cover versions and his own songs. Gary Barlow is one of Britain's most successful songwriter having written fourteen number-one singles and twenty-four top-ten hits. As solo artist he has had three number-one singles, six top-ten singles and two number-one albums, and has additionally had seventeen top-five hits, twelve number-one singles and eight number-one albums with Take That. In 2000, Barlow made his acting debut in the ITV1 drama Heartbeat: this was the 150t edition of the show, and Barlow played hitch-hiker Micky Shannon. In his autobiography My Take, Barlow revealed that he is a supporter of Liverpool F with their anthem "You'll Never Walk Alone" being one of the first songs he learned to play on the piano.

Clare Victoria Balding OBE was born on the 29th January 1971 and is a broadcaster, journalist and author. From 1988 to 1993, Balding was a leading amateur flat jockey and Champion Lady Rider in 1990. Clare Balding has close family links to horse racing: her father, Ian Balding, trained Mill Reef, 1971 winner of The Derby, Prix de l'Arc de Triomphe and King George VI and Queen Elizabeth Stakes; and her younger brother, Andrew Balding, trained Casual Look, the winner of the 2003 Epsom Oaks. Clare Balding has reported from six Olympic Games, for BBC Radio in Atlanta and for BBC Television in Sydney, Athens, Beijing, London and Rio de Janeiro. She has presented four Paralympic Games, the Winter Olympics from Salt Lake City, Turin, Vancouver and Sochi as well as the Commonwealth Games from Melbourne, Delhi and Glasgow. She was the face of the BBC's rugby league coverage, having presented Grandstand from a Rugby League Challenge Cup semi-final, and having been so impressed by the vibrancy and physical challenge of the sport she asked to cover further rugby league events. She was the last person to present Sunday Grandstand.

manda Louise Holden was born on the 16th February 1971 is an English media ersonality, actress, television presenter, singer and author. Although born in ortsmouth, Amanda Holden spent much of her childhood in Bishop's Waltham nd, at age 9 she joined Bishop's Waltham Little Theatre Company. Amanda olden's first television appearance was as a contestant on the game show Blind ate in 1991. Amanda is currently a judge on Britain's Got Talent along with mon Cowell, David Walliams, and Alesha Dixon. She joined the show in 2007. n the 13th April 2008, Holden ran the London Marathon in 4 hours and 13 inutes, in the name of the Born Free Foundation, having collected public and elebrity sponsors online. In 2010 Holden campaigned to keep a Sainsbury's upermarket out of Bishop's Waltham. Residents of her hometown later accused er of a double standard in November 2010 when she signed a deal to appear in dvertisements for Tesco, the UK's largest supermarket chain. Since 2013, Holden as presented the RSPCA's Animal Hero Awards. In 2019 she was awarded Rear the Year by the Daily Mirror newspaper.

Kirstie Mary Allsopp was born on the 31st August 1971 and is a British television presenter. She is best known as co-presenter of Channel 4 property shows including Location, Location, Location, Love It or List It UK, Relocation, Relocation and Location Revisited. She attended ten schools as a child included St Clotilde's in Lechlade, Gloucestershire and Bedales, near Petersfield, Hampshire. After spending time in India teaching English, Allsopp returned to the UK and began a series of positions, working for Country Living and Food & Homes Magazine and her mother's business, Hindlip & Prentice Interiors, and studying at Christie's. Allsopp set up her own home search company, Kirmir, in 1996, focusing on top end purchases in Central and West London. In 2009 they, along with another family, bought and restored a house in rural Devon called Meadowgate, which had been empty for 39 years. The restoration and interior decorating was the subject of the series "Kirstie's Homemade Home". It was again the setting for her "Kirstie's Homemade Christmas" programme showing people how to have an individual Christmas using second-hand and homemade products.

George Gideon Oliver Osborne born on the 23rd May 1971 is a British newspap editor and former Conservative Party politician. Between 1995 and 1997 he worked as a special adviser to the Minister of Agriculture, Fisheries and Food Douglas Hogg (during the BSE crisis), and in the Political Office at 10 Downing Street. Osborne worked on Prime Minister John Major's campaign team in 199 in the run-up to the Tories' heavy election defeat that year. After the election, he again considered journalism, approaching The Times to be a leader writer, though nothing came of it. Between 1997 and 2001 he worked for William Hague, Major's successor as Conservative Party leader, as a speechwriter and political secretary. Osborne was appointed Chancellor of the Exchequer on 11 May 2010, and was sworn in as a Privy Counsellor the following day. After the Conservatives won an overall majority at the 2015 general election, Osborne w reappointed Chancellor of the Exchequer by Cameron in his second governmen Osborne also received the honorific title of First Secretary of State.

Howard Melton Webb, MBE was born on the 14th July 1971 and was an English former professional football referee. Howard Webb is counted amongst the all-time top referees by the International Federation of Football History and Statistics and refereed a number of notable matches in England including the FA Cup final, the FA Community Shield and the final of the League Cup. In 2010, he became the first person to referee the finals of both the UEFA Champions League and FIFA World Cup in the same year. Throughout his professional career, Webb drew praise for his authoritative and respected approach to refereeing from football bodies, pundits, colleagues, players and managers. He announced his retirement in August 2014 to become the technical director of the Professional Game Match Officials Board. On the 6th August 2014, the Premier League announced that Webb had retired from active refereeing in order to take up the role of technical director of the Professional Game Match Officials Board. He began his career in policing in 1993 and took a five-year career break in 2008 to focus on refereeing. He returned to the South Yorkshire Police in April 2013.

Karen Jane Wallace born on the 25th September 1971, known professionally Jessie Wallace, is an English actress. After schooling, Karen trained as a make-up artist at the College of North East London in Tottenham and worked at the Royal Shakespeare Company for two years. Her first television appearance wa in an episode of the ITV police drama series The Bill in 1999. Karen is best known for playing the role of Kat Slater in BBC One soap opera EastEnders between 2000 and 2005. In February 2010 it was announced that Shane Richi was returning to play Alfie Moon, leading to large amounts of speculation as whether Wallace would also be returning. On the 9th February 2010, the BBC confirmed that Jessie would be returning to EastEnders, reprising her role as Kat Slater. During her break from EastEnders, Wallace made television guest appearances, including once as Kat Slater, in the 2005 French & Saunders Christmas special. On the 4th April 2015, the BBC announced that Wallace and Richie will depart from the show temporarily to appear in a six-part BBC One drama series, Red water.

Kyran Paul Patrick Bracken MBE born 22nd November 1971 in Dublin, Ireland and is a world-cup winning former rugby union footballer. Kyran Bracken made his England debut in November 1993 against the All Blacks. However, a stamp from Jamie Joseph seriously injured his ankle, putting him out of action for three months and leaving him with a permanent weakness. Bracken joined Saracens in 1996 and was part of the team that won the Tetley's Bitter Cup against Wasps in 1998. He missed out on selection for the 1997 British and Irish Lions tour to South Africa in favour of Matt Dawson and Austin Healey, but was called up as injury replacement for Rob Howley but did not play in the tests. Kyran Bracken starred in and won ITV's celebrity ice dancing competition Dancing on Ice in 2007, with partner Melanie Lambert and won the final on the 17th March 2007 after a performance which included the required element of "flying" on wires and a final performance of Bolero. Kyran Bracken is an Honorary President of the rugby charity Wooden Spoon improving the lives of disadvantaged children and young people in Britain and Ireland.

Emily Kathleen Anne Mortimer was born on the 1st December 1971 and is an English actress and screenwriter. Emily Mortimer performed in several plays while studying at University of Oxford. While acting in a student production, she was spotted by a producer who later cast her in the lead in a television adaptation of Catherine Cookson's The Glass Virgin (1995). Subsequent television roles included Sharpe's Sword (1995) and Coming Home (1998). In 2000, Emily was cast as Katherine in Kenneth Branagh's musical adaptation of Love's Labour's Lost, where she met actor and future husband Alessandro Nivola. She took on her biggest role in an American film to date, playing opposite Bruce Willis in Disney's The Kid. Emily Mortimer played an aspiring actress opposite Andy García in City Island (2009) and as Rachel Solando in Martin Scorsese's 2010 film Shutter Island. In 2000, Emily met American actor Alessandro Nivola while both were starring in Love's Labour's Lost. The couple married in the village of Turville in the Chilterns, Buckinghamshire, on the 3rd January 2003.

Dido Florian Cloud de Bounevialle O'Malley Armstrong was born on the 25th December 1971, known professionally as Dido she is an English singer and songwriter. Dido attained international success with her debut album No Angel (1999). Hit singles from the album include "Here with Me" and "Thank You". It sold over 21 million copies worldwide, and won her several awards, including two Brit Awards: Best British Female and Best British Album, and the MTV Europe Music Award for Best New Act. Dido's first two albums are among the best-selling albums in UK chart history, and both are in the top 10 best-selling albums of the 2000s in the UK. Dido made a comeback in 2013, releasing her fourth studio album Girl Who Got Away, which reached the top 5 in the UK. Having taken time out of the music industry to raise her son, she reappeared on stage at the 2013 Reading and Leeds festival where she reunited with Eminem. In 2018, Dido announced her first tour in 15 years in support of her new album, Still on My Mind, that was released on the 8th March 2019.

BRITISH DEATHS

Admiral of the Fleet John Cronyn Tovey, 1st Baron Tovey, GCB, KBE, DSO Born 7th March 1885 – 12th January 1971, sometimes known as Jack Tovey, was a Royal Navy officer. During the First World War he commanded the destroyer HMS Onslow at the Battle of Jutland and then commanded the destroyer Ursa at the Second Battle of Heligoland Bight. During the Second World War he initially served as Second-in-Command of the Mediterranean Fleet in which role he commanded the Mediterranean Fleet's Light Forces (i.e. cruisers and destroyers). He then served as Commander-in-Chief of the Home Fleet and was responsible for orchestrating the pursuit and destruction of the Bismarck. After that he became Commander-in-Chief, The Nore with responsibility for controlling the east coast convoys and organising minesweeping operations. Tovey retired from the service early in 1946 and was ennobled as Baron Tovey, of Langton Matravers in the County of Dorset on 15 February 1946. He died at Funchal, Madeira on the 12th January 1971.

Violet Constance Jessop born 2nd October 1887 – 5th May 1971. She was an Irish Argentine ocean liner stewardess and nurse. In 1911, Jessop began working as a stewardess for the White Star vessel RMS Olympic. Olympic was a luxury ship that was the largest civilian liner at that time. Jessop was on board on the 20th September 1911, when Olympic left from Southampton and collided with the British warship HMS Hawke. Jessop boarded RMS Titanic as a stewardess on the 10th April 1912, at age 24. Four days later, on the 14th April, it struck an iceberg in the North Atlantic, where Titanic sank about two hours and forty minutes after the collision. During the First World War, Jessop served as a stewardess for the British Red Cross. On the morning of the 21st November 1916, she was on board HMHS Britannic, a White Star liner that had been converted into a hospital ship, when it sank in the Aegean Sea due to an unexplained explosion. Jessop, often winkingly called "Miss Unsinkable", died of congestive heart failure in 1971 at the age of 83.

Dame Gladys Constance Cooper, DBE born 18th December 1888 – 17th November 1971 and was an English actress whose career spanned seven decades on stage, in films and on television. As a teenager in Edwardian musical comedy and pantomime, she starred in dramatic roles and silent films before the First World War. She managed the Playhouse Theatre from 1917 to 1933, where she played many roles. From the early 1920s Cooper won praise in plays by W. Somerset Maugham and others.

In the 1930s she starred steadily in productions both in London's West End and on Broadway. Moving to Hollywood in 1940, Cooper found success in a variety of character roles. She received three Academy Award nominations for Best Supporting Actress, for performances in The Song of Bernadette (1943), My Fair Lady (1964) and, most famously, Now, Voyager (1942). Throughout the 1950s and 60s she worked both on stage and on screen, continuing to star on stage until her last year.

SPORTING EVENTS 1971

1971 County Cricket Season

The 1971 County Championship was the 72nd officially organised running of the County Championship. Surrey won the Championship title by virtue of winning more matches because they had finished level on points with Warwickshire. The club's home ground is The Oval, in the Kennington area of Lambeth in South London. They have been based there continuously since 1845. The club also has an 'out ground' at Woodbridge Road, Guildford, where some home games are played each season. Surrey have won the County Championship 19 times outright (and shared once), a number exceeded only by Yorkshire, with their most recent win being in 2018. The club's badge is the Prince of Wales's feathers, used since 1915, as the Prince of Wales owns the land on which The Oval stands. The club is associated with the colour chocolate brown, wearing brown caps and helmets, and is sometimes known by the nickname 'Brown Caps'.

County Championship table							
Team	Pld	Won	Lost	Drawn	Batting bonus	Bowling bonus	Points
Surrey	24	11	3	10	63	82	255
Warwickshire	24	9	9	6	73	92	255
Lancashire	24	9	4	11	76	75	241
Kent	24	7	6	11	82	82	234
Leicestershire	24	6	2	16	76	74	215
Middlesex	24	7	6	11	61	81	212
Somerset	24	7	4	13	50	89	209
Gloucestershire	24	7	3	13	50	81	201
Hampshire	24	4	6	14	70	82	192
Essex	24	6	5	13	43	84	187
Sussex	24	5	9	10	55	77	182
Nottinghamshire	24	3	7	14	58	83	171
Yorkshire	24	4	8	12	47	75	162
Northamptonshire	24	4	8	12	36	83	159
Worcestershire	24	3	7	14	46	76	152
Glamorgan	24	3	5	15	55	63	148
Derbyshire	24	1	4	19	51	81	142

1970–71 in English football

The 1970–71 season was the 91st season of competitive football in England. Arsenal won the league championship at the end of a season which would soon be followed by their FA Cup final tie with Liverpool. Arsenal secured the league title at White Hart Lane, the home of bitter rivals Tottenham. They narrowly overcame Leeds to win the league, with a 12-point gap separating Leeds from third-placed Tottenham. Wolves and Liverpool joined these two teams in the UEFA Cup. Chelsea missed out on the top five on goal average but compensated for this shortcoming by achieving European Cup Winners' Cup glory over Real Madrid.

Pos	Team	Pld	W	D	L	GF	GA	GR	Pts	Qualification or relegation
1	Arsenal	42	29	7	6	71	29	2.448	65	Qualified for the European Cup
2	Leeds United	42	27	10	5	72	30	2.400	64	
3	Tottenham Hotspur	42	19	14	9	54	33	1.636	52	Qualified for the UEFA Cup
4	Wolverhampton Wanderers	42	22	8	12	64	54	1.185	52	
5	Liverpool	42	17	17	8	42	24	1.750	51	Qualified for the Cup Winners' Cup
6	Chelsea	42	18	15	9	52	42	1.238	51	
7	Southampton	42	17	12	13	56	44	1.273	46	Qualified for the UEFA Cup
8	Manchester United	42	16	11	15	65	66	0.985	43	
9	Derby County	42	16	10	16	56	54	1.037	42	
10	Coventry City	42	16	10	16	37	38	0.974	42	
11	Manchester City	42	12	17	13	47	42	1.119	41	
12	Newcastle United	42	14	13	15	44	46	0.957	41	
13	Stoke City	42	12	13	17	44	48	0.917	37	
14	Everton	42	12	13	17	54	60	0.900	37	
15	Huddersfield Town	42	11	14	17	40	49	0.816	36	
16	Nottingham Forest	42	14	8	20	42	61	0.689	36	
17	West Bromwich Albion	42	10	15	17	58	75	0.773	35	
18	Crystal Palace	42	12	11	19	39	57	0.684	35	
19	Ipswich Town	42	12	10	20	42	48	0.875	34	
20	West Ham United	42	10	14	18	47	60	0.783	34	
21	Burnley	42	7	13	22	29	63	0.460	27	Relegated to the Second Division
22	Blackpool	42	4	15	23	34	66	0.515	23	

1970–71 Scottish Division One

The 1970–71 season was the 98th season of competitive football in Scotland and the 74th season of Scottish league football. Aberdeen, with a 15-game unbeaten run, led the league from December until the last week of the season. Aberdeen faced Celtic in their penultimate game, needing a win to almost certainly clinch the title, but could only draw 1–1 and then they lost their last game, at Falkirk, allowing Celtic to take the championship by 2 points.

Celtic are one of only five clubs in the world (which also includes their rivals Rangers) to have won over 100 trophies in their history. The club has won the Scottish League championship 50 times, most recently in 2018–19, the Scottish Cup 39 times and the Scottish League Cup 19 times.

Division 1

Pos	Team	Pld	W	D	L	GF	GA	GD	Pts	Qualification or relegation
1	Celtic	34	25	6	3	89	23	+66	56	Champion
2	Aberdeen	34	24	6	4	68	18	+50	54	
3	St Johnstone	34	19	6	9	59	44	+15	44	
4	Rangers	34	16	9	9	58	34	+24	41	
5	Dundee	34	14	10	10	53	45	+8	38	
6	Dundee United	34	14	8	12	53	54	−1	36	
7	Falkirk	34	13	9	12	46	53	−7	35	
8	Morton	34	13	8	13	44	44	0	34	
9	Airdrieonians	34	13	8	13	60	65	−5	34	
10	Motherwell	34	13	8	13	43	47	−4	34	
11	Heart of Midlothian	34	13	7	14	41	40	+1	33	
12	Hibernian	34	10	10	14	47	53	−6	30	
13	Kilmarnock	34	10	8	16	43	67	−24	28	
14	Ayr United	34	9	8	17	37	54	−17	26	
15	Clyde	34	8	10	16	33	59	−26	26	
16	Dunfermline Athletic	34	6	11	17	44	56	−12	23	
17	St Mirren	34	7	9	18	38	56	−18	23	Relegated to 1971–72 Second Division
18	Cowdenbeath	34	7	3	24	33	69	−36	17	

1971 Five Nations Championship

The 1971 Five Nations Championship was the forty-second series of the rugby union Five Nations Championship. Including the previous incarnations as the Home Nations and Five Nations, this was the seventy-seventh series of the northern hemisphere rugby union championship. This was the last Five Nations tournament where a try was worth 3 points. Ten matches were played between 16th January and 27th March. It was contested by England, France, Ireland, Scotland and Wales.

Wales won all their four matches to win the championship for the seventeenth time outright, excluding shared titles. They won the Triple Crown for the second time in three seasons and the twelfth time overall and completed the Grand Slam for the first time since 1952 and the sixth time overall.

Table

Position	Nation	Games				Points			Table points
		Played	Won	Drawn	Lost	For	Against	Difference	
1	Wales	4	4	0	0	73	38	+35	8
2	France	4	1	2	1	41	40	+1	4
3	Ireland	4	1	1	2	41	46	−5	3
3	England	4	1	1	2	44	58	−14	3
5	Scotland	4	1	0	3	47	64	−17	2

Results

France	13–8	Scotland
Wales	22–6	England
Ireland	6–9	England
Scotland	18–19	Wales
England	14–14	France
Scotland	5–17	Ireland
Wales	23–9	Ireland
England	15–16	Scotland
France	5–9	Wales
Ireland	9–9	France

The Masters 1971

The 1971 Masters Tournament was the 35th Masters Tournament, held April 8–11 at Augusta National Golf Club in Augusta, Georgia. Charles Coody won his only major championship, two strokes ahead of runners-up Johnny Miller and Jack Nicklaus.

Miller was six-under for the Sunday round and, playing two groups ahead of the final two-some, his birdie on 14 would open up a two-shot lead when Coody subsequently bogeyed the hole, but could not hold on to win. Coody, co-leader with Nicklaus entering the round, rebounded from his bogey at 14 with two consecutive birdies and parred the final two holes while Miller, 23, bogeyed two of the last three holes. It was a bit of redemption for Coody, who bogeyed the final three holes in 1969 to finish two strokes back. It was Coody's third and final win on the PGA Tour.

Future 3-time U.S. Open champion Hale Irwin made his Masters debut in 1971 and tied for 13th place. It was the final Masters for two champions: 1948 winner Claude Harmon withdrew during the first round and 1955 champion Cary Middlecoff during the second. Dave Stockton won the twelfth Par 3 contest on Wednesday with a score of 23. For the only time in its history, the Masters was not the first major championship of the year. The 1971 PGA Championship was played in Florida in February, and was won by Nicklaus. The co-leader entering Sunday, his attempt to secure the second leg of the grand slam came up short on the back nine on Sunday, as he shot 37 for an even-par 72.

Place	Player	Country	Score	To par	Money ($)
1	**Charles Coody**	United States	66-73-70-70=279	−9	25,000
T2	Johnny Miller	United States	72-73-68-68=281	−7	17,500
	Jack Nicklaus	United States	70-71-68-72=281		
T4	Don January	United States	69-69-73-72=283	−5	9,050
	Gene Littler	United States	72-69-73-69=283		
T6	Gary Player	South Africa	72-72-71-69=284	−4	5,600
	Ken Still	United States	72-71-72-69=284		
	Tom Weiskopf	United States	71-69-72-72=284		
T9	Frank Beard	United States	74-73-69-70=286	−2	3,767
	Roberto DeVicenzo	Argentina	76-69-72-69=286		
	Dave Stockton	United States	72-73-69-72=286		

Augusta National Golf Club, sometimes referred to as Augusta or the National, is one of the most famous and exclusive golf clubs in the world, located in Augusta, Georgia, United States. Unlike most private clubs which operate as non-profits, Augusta National is a for-profit corporation, and it does not disclose its income, holdings, membership list, or ticket sales. Founded by Bobby Jones and Clifford Roberts, the course was designed by Jones and Alister Mackenzie and opened for play in 1932. Since 1934, the club has played host to the annual Masters tournament, one of the four major championships in professional golf, and the only major played each year at the same course. It was the top-ranked course in Golf Digest's 2009 list of America's 100 greatest courses and was the number ten-ranked course based on course architecture on Golf week Magazine's 2011 list of best classic courses in the United States.

Grand National 1971

The Grand National is a National Hunt horse race held annually at Aintree Racecourse, near Liverpool, England. First run in 1839, it is a handicap steeplechase over an official distance of about 4 miles and 2½ furlongs, (or accurately 4 miles 514 yards (6.907 km)); with horses jumping 30 fences over two laps. It is the most valuable jump race in Europe, with a prize fund of £1 million in 2017. The 1971 Grand National was the 125th renewal of the Grand National horse race that took place at Aintree near Liverpool, England, on the 3rd April 1971. Gay Buccaneer was very unlucky having been the clear leader at the Canal turn on the first circuit, only to be interfered with by a loose horse which resulted in him going from first to last, and finishing tenth. Specify was the winner from a close finish between the leading five in the final furlong.

Triple Crown Winners 1971

2,000 Guineas

Brigadier Gerard wins 2000 Guineas. The field of six runners for the season's first colts' classic, the 2000 Guineas at Newmarket, was one of the smallest in recent memory. However, the three colts that had headed the Free handicap, My Swallow, Mill Reef, and Brigadier Gerard, had between them won 18 of their 19 races, including every major two-year-old race in Europe. My Swallow and Mill Reef had won their prep races, the Usher Stakes and the Greenham Stakes, while Brigadier Gerard, as planned, arrived at the Rowley Mile without a preparatory race. The race was generally billed as a match between the 6/4 favourite Mill Reef and the 2/1 second favourite My Swallow. Brigadier Gerard was relatively overlooked at 11/2, Minsky, a full brother to Nijinsky and Irish champion 2-y-o in 1970 at 15/2, Good Bond at 16/1 and Indian Ruler the complete outsider at 100/1.

St Leger

Athens Wood wins St Leger. He made his racing debut as a two-year-old in July 1970. He won three starts in England including the Solario Stakes then was sent to France to compete where he ran sixth in a Grade II event at Maisons-Laffitte Racecourse. Ridden by Greville Starkey, Athens Wood made a winning debut as a three-year-old on the 4th June 1971 then won his next start at Epsom Downs before finishing third to winner Homeric in the Lingfield Derby Trial. In July he won the Gordon Stakes at Goodwood Racecourse and then in August captured the Great Voltigeur Stakes at York Racecourse. In September, Athens Wood won the most important race of his career at Doncaster Racecourse when Lester Piggott rode him to victory in the Classic St. Leger Stakes.

The Derby

Mill Reef wins the Epsom Derby. As a three-year-old, following a victory in the Greenham Stakes at Newbury, Mill Reef was beaten three lengths in the 2,000 Guineas by Brigadier Gerard, who was to prove himself one of the best milers ever, with his old rival My Swallow back in third. Although his breeding hinted otherwise, Mill Reef then proved himself to be the outstanding middle distance racehorse of the year, winning The Derby by two lengths from Linden Tree, the Eclipse Stakes at Sandown (beating the crack French colt Caro by four lengths) and the King George VI and Queen Elizabeth Stakes at Ascot by six lengths from Derby Italiano winner Ortis. In October, he was victorious in the Prix de l'Arc de Triomphe at Longchamp in France, beating the star French filly Pistol Packer by three lengths.

1971 British Grand Prix

The 1971 British Grand Prix was a Formula One motor race held at Silverstone on the 17th July 1971. It was race 6 of 11 in both the 1971 World Championship of Drivers and the 1971 International Cup for Formula One Manufacturers. The 68-lap race was won by Tyrrell driver Jackie Stewart after he started from second position. Ronnie Peterson finished second for the March team and Lotus driver Emerson Fittipaldi came in third. On one of the fastest circuits on the calendar, horsepower counted for everything. Clay Regazzoni, driving for Ferrari, gained pole with a scorching lap of 1 min 18.1 secs, beating Jackie Stewart in a Tyrrell and Jo Siffert in a BRM by just a couple of hundredths of a second.

Final Placings

Pos	No	Driver	Constructor	Laps	Time/Retired	Grid	Points
1	12	Jackie Stewart	Tyrrell-Ford	68	1:31:31.5	2	9
2	18	Ronnie Peterson	March-Ford	68	+ 36.1	5	6
3	1	Emerson Fittipaldi	Lotus-Ford	68	+ 50.5	4	4
4	26	Henri Pescarolo	March-Ford	67	+ 1 Lap	17	3
5	24	Rolf Stommelen	Surtees-Ford	67	+ 1 Lap	12	2
6	23	John Surtees	Surtees-Ford	67	+ 1 Lap	18	1
7	22	Jean-Pierre Beltoise	Matra	66	+ 2 Laps	15	
8	17	Howden Ganley	BRM	66	+ 2 Laps	11	
9	16	Jo Siffert	BRM	66	+ 2 laps	3	
10	14	François Cevert	Tyrrell-Ford	65	+ 3 Laps	10	

he start itself was a shambles, with a bungled flag drop causing a collision between Jackie Oliver and Graham lill, for which Oliver was fined £50. Regazzoni led away from Jacky Ickx and Stewart, but after just one lap tewart had passed Ickx, with Siffert following him. On lap 4, Stewart passed Regazzoni and disappeared into the listance. By lap 10 he was over 3 seconds ahead. In the point's positions, Emerson Fittipaldi, Ronnie Peterson and im Schenken were having a memorable tussle. Regazzoni repassed Siffert who was suffering from vibration roblems on lap 15, but the BRM driver managed to hang on to the back of the Ferrari for several more laps. tewart increased his lead to 14 seconds and by lap 20 he was ahead by 18 seconds. Ickx dropped out of fourth lace with rubber breaking off from his front left tyre, and Siffert dropped way down with a broken coil bracket. he battle between Peterson, Schenken and Fittipaldi moved up into 3rd, 4th and 5th places.

ackie Stewart took a commanding home win and extended his lead in the Championship to 23 points.

1971 Wimbledon Championships

The 1971 Wimbledon Championships was a tennis tournament that took place on the outdoor grass courts at the All England Lawn Tennis and Croquet Club in Wimbledon, London, United Kingdom. The tournament was held from Monday 21 June until Saturday 3rd July 1971. It was the 85th staging of the Wimbledon Championships, and the third Grand Slam tennis event of 1971. John Newcombe and Evonne Goolagong won the singles titles.

Men's Singles

John Newcombe successfully defended his title, defeating Stan Smith in the final, 6–3, 5–7, 2–6, 6–4, and 6–4 to win the Gentlemen's Singles tennis title at the 1971 Wimbledon Championships. It was Newcombe's third, and final, Wimbledon singles title.

Women's Singles

Evonne Goolagong defeated the defending champion Margaret Court in the final, 6–4, and 6–1 to win the Ladies' Singles tennis title at the 1971 Wimbledon Championships.

Men's Doubles

John Newcombe and Tony Roche were the defending champions, but lost in the first round to Cliff Drysdale and Nikola Pilić. Roy Emerson and Rod Laver defeated Arthur Ashe and Dennis Ralston in the final, 4–6, 9–7, 6–8, 6–4, 6–4 to win the Gentlemen's Doubles title at the 1971 Wimbledon Championships.

Women's Doubles

Rosie Casals and Billie Jean King successfully defended their title, defeating Margaret Court and Evonne Goolagong in the final, 6–3, 6–2 to win the Ladies' Doubles tennis title at the 1971 Wimbledon Championships

Mixed Doubles

Ilie Năstase and Rosie Casals were the defending champions, but lost in the semi-finals to Owen Davidson and Billie Jean King. Davidson and King defeated Marty Riessen and Margaret Court in the final, 3–6, 6–2, 15–13 to win the Mixed Doubles tennis title at the 1971 Wimbledon Championships.

John Newcombe

Evonne Goolagong

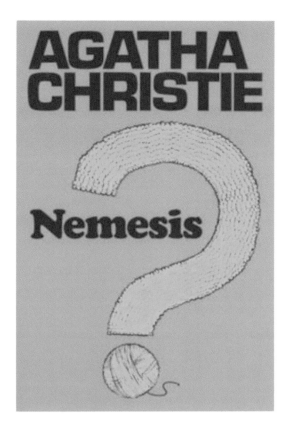

emesis is a work of detective fiction by Agatha Christie (1890–1976) ad first published in the UK by the Collins Crime Club in November 971. Miss Marple receives a letter from the solicitors of the recently eceased Jason Rafiel, a millionaire whom she had met during a oliday on which she had encountered a murder, which asks her to ok into an unspecified crime; if she succeeds in solving the crime, ne will inherit £20,000. Rafiel has left her few clues. She begins by ining a tour of famous British houses and gardens with fifteen other eople, arranged by Mr Rafiel prior to his death. Elizabeth Temple is e retired school headmistress who relates the story of Verity, who as engaged to Rafiel's ne'er-do-well son, Michael, but the marriage d not happen. Another member of the tour group, Miss Cooke, is a oman she had met briefly in St Mary Mead. Her next clue comes om Lavinia Glynne; Rafiel had written to Mrs Glynne and her two sters before his death, suggesting Miss Marple spend the most nysically challenging few days of the tour with them. Miss Marple ccepts Lavinia's invitation. She then meets Lavinia's spinster sisters, otilde and Anthea Bradbury-Scott. On talking with the servant, Miss larple learns Verity joined the family after both her parents died, ecoming quite attached to Clotilde. Verity is dead now, brutally urdered. Michael Rafiel is in prison.

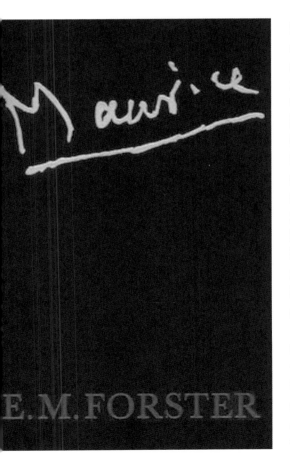

Maurice is a novel by E. M. Forster. A tale of homosexual love in early 20th-century England, it follows Maurice Hall from his schooldays through university and beyond. It was written in 1913–1914, and revised in 1932 and 1959–1960. Forster was close friends with the poet Edward Carpenter, and upon visiting his Derbyshire home in 1912, was motivated to write Maurice. The relationship between Carpenter and his partner, George Merrill, was the inspiration for that of Maurice and Alec Scudder. Although Forster showed the novel to a select few of his friends (among them Christopher Isherwood), it was published only posthumously, in 1971. Forster did not seek to publish it during his lifetime, believing it to have been unpublishable during that period due to public and legal attitudes to same-sex love. A note found on the manuscript read: "Publishable, but worth it?" Forster was particularly keen that his novel should have a happy ending, but knew that this would make the book too controversial.

In the original manuscripts, Forster wrote an epilogue concerning the post-novel fate of Maurice and Alec that he later discarded, because it was unpopular among those to whom he showed it. This epilogue can still be found in the Abinger edition of the novel. This edition also contains a summary of the differences between various versions of the novel.

The Day of the Jackal (1971) is a thriller novel by English author Frederick Forsyth about a professional assassin who is contracted by the OAS, a French dissident paramilitary organisation, to kill Charles de Gaulle, the President of France. The book begins in 1962 with the (historical) failed attempt on de Gaulle's life planned by Col. Jean-Marie Bastien-Thiry in the Paris suburb of Petit-Clamart: Operation Charlotte Corday. Following the arrest of Bastien-Thiry and remaining conspirators, the French security forces wage a short but extremely vicious "underground" war with the terrorists of the OAS, a militant right-wing group who have labelled de Gaulle a traitor to France after his grant of independence to Algeria. The French secret service, particularly its covert operations directorate is remarkably effective in infiltrating the terrorist organisation with their own informants, allowing them to seize and interrogate the terrorists' operations commander, Antoine Argoud. The failure of the Petit-Clamart assassination, and a subsequent unsuccessful attempt at the École Militaire, compounded by Bastien-Thiry's eventual execution by firing squad, likewise demoralise the antagonists. The novel received admiring reviews and praise when first published in 1971, and it received a 1972 Best Novel Edgar Award from the Mystery Writers of America.

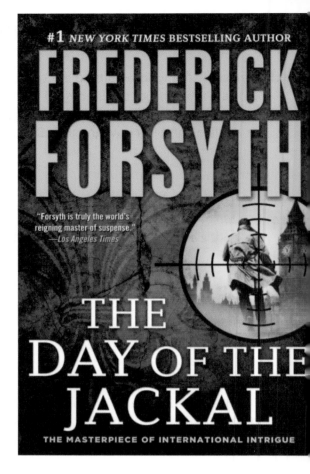

#1 *NEW YORK TIMES* BESTSELLING AUTHOR

FREDERICK FORSYTH

"Forsyth is truly the world's reigning master of suspense."
—*Los Angeles Times*

THE DAY OF THE JACKAL

THE MASTERPIECE OF INTERNATIONAL INTRIGUE

MR. TICKLE
By Roger Hargreaves

MR. MEN
LITTLE MISS

Mr. Men is a series of children's books by English author Roger Hargreaves commencing in 1971. From 1981, an accompanying series of Little Miss books by the same author, but with female characters were published. A similar series of animal characters known as Timbuctoo started in 1978. After Hargreaves's death in 1988, his son Adam Hargreaves began writing and illustrating new Mr. Men and Little Miss stories like Mr. Good, Mr. Cool, Mr. Rude, Little Miss Scary, Little Miss Bad and Little Miss Whoops.

Each book in the original Mr. Men and Little Miss series introduce a different title character and his/her single dominant personality trait to convey a simple moral lesson. The Mr. Men and Little Miss characters frequently reappeared in other characters' books. As of 2015, a total of 85 Mr. Men and Little Miss characters had been featured in the series. The books' simple stories, with brightly coloured, boldly drawn illustrations, made them very popular, with sales of over 100 million worldwide across 28 countries.

The first six Mr. Men books were published in United Kingdom in 1971, priced at 20p each. Mr. Tickle was the first Mr. Men character created by Hargreaves, inspired by his son, Adam, who had asked him what a tickle looked like. Hargreaves responded with a round, orange figure with long, bendy arms.

Adolf Hitler: My Part in His Downfall, published in 1971, is the first volume of Spike Milligan's war memoirs. The book spans the period from Britain's declaration of war on Germany to when Milligan lands in Algeria as a part of the Allied liberation of Africa. The preface anticipates the book will be part of a trilogy; years later, the cover of the fourth volume said: "Don't be fooled this is the last, volume four of the war memoirs." Ultimately, however, Milligan published seven volumes covering his war service, his first nervous breakdown and reallocation to rear-echelon duties, his demob and early years trying to break into the entertainment industry. In Mussolini: His Part in My Downfall, having been stung by a critic who called the biographies unreliable, Milligan wrote, "I wish the reader to know that he is not reading a tissue of lies and fancies, it all really happened." The presentation is an unusual format freely mixing narrative anecdotes, contemporary photography, excerpts from diaries, letters, rough sketches and performance programs, along with comic sketches and absurd fake memoranda from ranking Nazi officials; the hard facts are usually apparent. Milligan says in the preface: "All the salient facts are true"; at the end of the preface: "There were the deaths of some of my friends, and therefore, no matter how funny I tried to make this book, that will always be at the back of my mind: but, were they alive today, they would have been the first to join in the laughter.

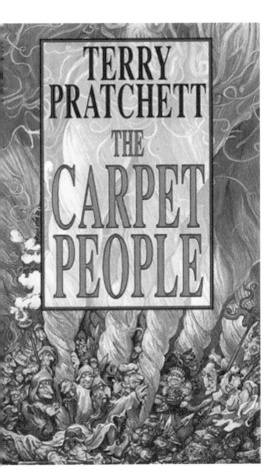

The Carpet People is a comic fantasy novel by British writer Terry Pratchett. First published in 1971, it was later re-written by the author when his work became more widespread and well-known. In the Author's Note of the revised edition, published in 1992, Pratchett wrote: "This book had two authors, and they were both the same person."

The Carpet People contains much of the humour and some of the concepts which later became a major part of the Discworld series, as well as parodies of everyday objects from our world. Before creating the Discworld, Pratchett wrote about two different flat worlds, first in this novel, and then in the novel Strata.

The book explores the conflict between traditions and innovation. There is an established civilization, complete with bureaucrats, taxes imposed and collected, and permits; there are people who resent the establishment; there is a need for both groups to find common ground in order to save their collective civilization.

Terry Pratchett's novel Eric mentions that the president of the demons has carpets inhabited by tribes of pygmies, possibly suggesting a link between The Carpet People and Discworld universes, or possibly merely one of Pratchett's in-jokes.

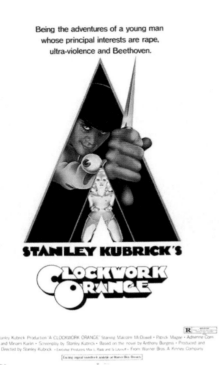

Being the adventures of a young man whose principal interests are rape, ultra-violence and Beethoven.

STANLEY KUBRICK'S
CLOCKWORK ORANGE

Clockwork Orange. In a near-futuristic society, late teen Alex DeLarge is the leader of a gang of thugs - his "droogs" - who commit acts of ultra-violence, often with sexual components, without any regard for their victims, and purely because it strikes their collective fancies. These acts are largely fuelled by drug use. In addition, Alex is a lover of music especially that of Ludwig van Beethoven, which, when he listens to it during these acts, intensifies his pleasure, and in turn inspires him to commit further such acts. He does not tolerate any challenge to his leadership by his droogs. Although the authorities in general know of Alex's delinquency, they have so far been unable to catch him in the act of his crimes, until one night after a sexual assault of an older woman. Alex and Alex alone is charged, convicted and incarcerated. But Alex sees what he believes is an easy way out when the government looks for subjects to participate in a new rehabilitation therapy, the end result being release from prison after the two week therapy. The therapy ends up having consequences that Alex did not envision.

Run time is 2h 16mins

Trivia

Malcolm McDowell's eyes were anesthetized for the torture scenes so that he would film for periods of time without too much discomfort. Nevertheless his corneas got repeatedly scratched by the metal lid locks.

Alex performing "Singing in the Rain" as he attacks the writer and his wife was not scripted. Stanley Kubrick spent four days experimenting with this scene, finding it too conventional. Eventually he approached Malcolm McDowell and asked him if he could dance. They tried the scene again, this time with McDowell dancing and singing the only song he could remember. Kubrick was so amused that he swiftly bought the rights to "Singing in the Rain" for $10,000.

Stanley Kubrick had his assistant destroy all unused footage.

Goofs

There is a running theme of the Government referring to Citizens and the State, implying that Great Britain has abolished the monarchy in this "future". Yet the prison is called "HM Prison Parkmoor", HM being a common designation for Her/his Majesty.

In the music store, the camera is briefly reflected in the mirrors to the right.

Many of the continuity errors are not in fact errors. Stanley Kubrick purposely included many continuity errors as a way of creating a feeling of disorientation for the audience. That is why people's positions change, props are reorganized, and hats (and other articles of clothing) appear and disappear.

When the brutal police try to drown Alex in the water trough, you can tell that the water has been warmed because there is steam coming from it.

Willy Wonka and The Chocolate Factory. The world is astounded when Willy Wonka, for years a recluse in his factory, announces that five lucky people will be given a tour of the factory, shown all the secrets of his amazing candy, and one will win a lifetime supply of Wonka chocolate. Nobody wants the prize more than young Charlie, but as his family is so poor that buying even one bar of chocolate is a treat, buying enough bars to find one of the five golden tickets is unlikely in the extreme. But in movie land, magic can happen.

Charlie, along with four somewhat odious other children, get the chance of a lifetime and a tour of the factory. Along the way, mild disasters befall each of the odious children, but can Charlie beat the odds and grab the brass ring?

Oscar Nominee: Best Music, Scoring Adaptation and Original Song Score.
Golden Globes Nominee: Best Actor in a Motion Picture - Comedy or Musical Gene **Wilder.**

Run time 1h 40mins

Trivia

After reading the script, Gene Wilder said he would take the role of Willy Wonka under one condition: that he would be allowed to limp, and then suddenly somersault in the scene when he first meets the children. When director Mel Stuart asked why, Wilder replied that having Wonka do this meant that "from that time on, no one will know if I'm lying or telling the truth." Stuart asked, "If I say no, you won't do the picture?" and Wilder said I'm afraid that's the truth."

The chocolate river was made from 150,000 gallons of water, real chocolate and cream. Because of the cream it began to spoil and, by the end of filming, smelled terrible.

Gene Wilder's acting during the boat ride sequence was so convincing that it frightened some of the other actors and actresses, including Denise Nickerson (Violet). They thought that Wilder really was going mad from being in the tunnel.

Goofs

When Mr. Salt pleads with Veruca, he says four Golden Tickets remain to be found. However, he mouths "three" and holds up three fingers (at around 11 mins). The obvious audio dub indicates either an error, or that the filmmakers may have switched around the order in which the children are introduced during editing.

When Mr. Turkentine is giving the class a math lesson, he says that 100 is 10% of 1000 then says that 150 is 10% half over again, making that number 15% of 1000. Then he says that 200 are 15% half over again. 200 are 20% of 1000. If it were 15% half over again, it would be 22.5%, not 20%.

When Augustus is drinking from the chocolate river, you can see that the tunnel behind him has a noticeable black wall.

Diamonds Are Forever. When Bond investigates mysterious activities in the world diamond market, he discovers that the evil Ernst Blofeld is stockpiling the precious gems to use in a deadly laser satellite capable of destroying massive targets on land, sea, and air. Bond, with the help of beautiful smuggler Tiffany Case, sets out to stop the madman, but first he must grapple with a host of enemies. He confronts offbeat assassins Mr. Wint and Mr. Kidd, as well as Bambi and Thumper, two scantily-clad beauties who are more than a match for Bond in hand-to-hand combat. Finally, there's the reclusive billionaire Willard Whyte, who may just hold a vital clue to Blofeld's whereabouts.

Oscar Nominee: Best Sound

Box Office

Budget:$7,200,000 (estimated)
Gross USA: $43,819,547
Cumulative Worldwide Gross: $43,819,547

Run time 2h 01mins.

Trivia

Because of Sir Sean Connery's high fee, the special effects budget was significantly scaled back. Connery was reportedly paid one million two hundred fifty thousand dollars to return as James Bond, a figure unheard of in those days.

Since the car chase in Las Vegas would have many crashes, the filmmakers had an arrangement with Ford to use their vehicles. Ford's only demand was that Sir Sean Connery had to drive the 1971 Mustang Mach 1 that served as Tiffany Case's car.

Due to the height difference, Lana Wood had to stand on a box for most of her scenes with Sir Sean Connery. This proved to be problematic for the scene where Connery had to strip Lana out of her dress, and down to her underwear, because a body double would not have worked for obvious reasons. Ultimately, Lana was given extra high heels to wear in that scene.

Goofs

Secret Agents succeed best when they are still secret. Tiffany Case knows about James Bond even though she is just a diamond smuggler, which is a field far from the usual work of Special Branch. If he's achieved this level of fame, it's unlikely he'd be sent to infiltrate criminal organizations. In fact this recognition is a central plot line in The Man with the Golden Gun.

When Bond and Tiffany are eluding pursuers by driving down a narrow alley, they manage to tip their Mustang so it's balanced on its two right wheels, but when it emerges from the other end, it's on its two left wheels.

Bond is soaking wet when he gets out of the pool after fighting with Bambi and Thumper. He then walks down some stairs, and is dry before he reaches the bottom.

Fiddler on the Roof. At the beginning of the twentieth century, Jews and Orthodox Christians live in the little village of Anatevka in the pre-revolutionary Russia of the Czars. Among the traditions of the Jewish community, the matchmaker arranges the match and the father approves it. The milkman Reb Tevye is a poor man that has been married for twenty-five years with Golde and they have five daughters. When the local matchmaker Yente arranges the match between his older daughter Tzeitel and the old widow butcher Lazar Wolf, Tevye agrees with the wedding. However Tzeitel is in love with the poor tailor Motel Kamzoil and they ask permission to Tevye to get married that he accepts to please his daughter. Then his second daughter Hodel (Michele Marsh) and the revolutionary student Perchik decide to marry each other and Tevye is forced to accept. When Perchik is arrested by the Czar troops and sent to Siberia, Hodel decides to leave her family and homeland and travel to Siberia to be with her beloved Perchik. When his third daughter Chava decides to get married with the Christian Fyedka, Tevye does not accept and considers that Chava has died. Meanwhile the Czar troops evict the Jewish community from Anatevka.

Run time 3h 01mins

Trivia

The title comes from a painting by Russian artist Marc Chagall called "The Dead Man" which depicts a funeral scene and shows a man playing a violin on a rooftop. It is also used by Tevye in the story as a metaphor for trying to survive in a difficult, constantly changing world.

Before production, Norma Crane was diagnosed with breast cancer, which would eventually kill her. She told only director Norman Jewison; co-star Topol and associate producer Patrick J. Palmer, all of whom kept her secret.

The cart-horse, nicknamed "Shmuel" by the cast, was purchased from a lot destined for a Zagreb glue factory. After production Norman Jewison paid a local farmer to keep him for the rest of his natural life, which was another three years.

Goofs

When the fiddler is playing the first song, the movements of the fiddler's bow don't quite match up with the song.

When the old man is talking to Tevye about Tzeitel, the shadow of the microphone boom is visible on the old man's shirt.

When the family is preparing for the Sabbath, Golde tells Perchik to wash at the well, and she tells Hodel to help him. As they leave the room, Perchik goes out a side door and Hodel follows her sisters upstairs.

During the parade to Tzeitel and Motle's wedding with everyone holding candles, Yente's candle isn't burning.

Bedknobs and Broomsticks. London rascals Charlie (Ian Weighill), Paul (Roy Snart), and Carrie (Cindy O'Callaghan) are amongst a flood of kids evacuated to country villages, in their case, Pepperinge Eye, where a lack of host families means they're assigned "for now" to loner Miss Eglantine Price (Dame Angela Lansbury). They discover she's an apprentice witch by correspondence, and promise to keep her secret only if allowed to join the fun. Paul is given a spell to make the bed fly them anywhere by means of magical knob. Unwilling to miss out of the last spell, "substituary locomotion", they track down founding Professor Emelius Browne (David Tomlinson) in London. He's a crook who never believed his spells would work, but eagerly joins the band in the hunt for the other half of the magic book from which he borrowed, but "modernized". It means flying to the magical animal "Isle of Naboombu", in search of the powerful star of sorcerer Astoroth. It's to be put to use in the war effort, just in time as Germans land in the coastal town for a terror surprise mini-invasion, only to be fought off by a magical army.

Oscar winner: Best Effects, Special Visual Effects.

Run time 1h 57mins

Trivia

Julie Andrews initially turned down the role of Miss Eglantine Price. She eventually reconsidered, believing she owed her movie career to Walt Disney Studios and wanted to work there again. When she told the studio she'd changed her mind, Dame Angela Lansbury had already been cast.

Angela Lansbury hated what she called "by the numbers" acting in this movie. Due to the heavy special effects, the entire movie had to be storyboarded in advance, shot for shot. Every moment was pre-determined, and Lansbury wasn't free to explore her character naturally.

The opening credits sequence is homage to the Bayeux Tapestry, a seamless linen cloth made in France during medieval times that tells the story of the Norman conquest of England.

Goofs

When the market stall trader removes the necklace from around Carrie's neck, saying, "Who d'you think you are, the Queen of Sheba?" her mouth, reflected in the mirror, isn't moving.

Miss Price reads the instructions for Substituary Locomotion, gets as far as "five mystic words. These words are:" turns the page, and discovers that the rest of the book is missing. The end of that sentence should've been printed on the other side of the page she was holding.

The film starts with 'England in the August of 1940.' At the museum, the first woman taking evacuees says "anything to get these poor children away from those terrible bombings in London." The Battle of Britain was in full swing in August 1940, but London wasn't bombed until September 7th.

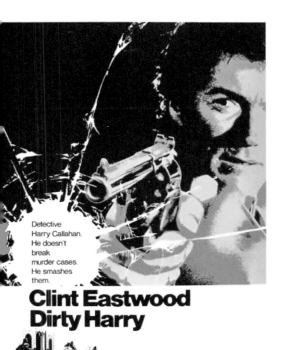

Detective
Harry Callahan.
He doesn't
break
murder cases.
He smashes
them.

Clint Eastwood
Dirty Harry

Dirty Harry. In 1971, San Francisco is under the terrorizing eye of a psychopathic sniper called the "Scorpio Killer" (Andrew Robinson), and claims in one of his written letters to the San Francisco Police Department that he will keep killing until his demands are made. Inspector "Dirty" Harry Callahan (Clint Eastwood) is a San Francisco police officer, with a dirty attitude, and uses little methods to what the law prescribes.

It becomes a menacing task for Callahan, as he's been assigned to apprehend the menacing killer at all costs, which later unravels into a cat-and-mouse game between the two men. One killer with a sinister, distasteful laughter. The other, a killer with just a plain dirty attitude who holds the badge.

Box Office

Budget:$4,000,000 (estimated)
Gross USA: $35,976,000
Cumulative Worldwide Gross: $35,976,000

Run time 1h 42mins

Trivia

Serial killer Scorpio was loosely based on the Zodiac killer, who used to taunt Police and media with notes about his crimes, in one of which he threatened to hijack a school bus full of children. The role of Harry Callahan was loosely based on real-life detective David Toschi, who was the chief investigator on the Zodiac case.

When Harry finally meets Scorpio in Mount Davidson Park, Scorpio orders him to show his gun with his left hand. Harry pulls it from his holster and Scorpio ad-libs the line, "My, that's a big one!" This line caused the crew to crack up and the scene had to be re-shot, but the line stayed.

Clint Eastwood performed all of his own stunts, including the stunt where he jumps onto the roof of the hijacked school bus from a bridge. His face is clearly visible throughout the shot.

Goofs

Before Harry clicks on the empty chamber for the bank robber, you hear and see him pull the hammer back to fire in single-action mode. However, when the camera faces Harry and he actually does pull the trigger, it is in double action, indicated by the fact that you see the cylinder spin again.

When Harry is following Scorpio's instructions to run from phone booth to phone booth, he boards the subway. When he arrives at his destination, it is the exact same station as the one where he boarded.

Callahan finds the note at the beginning stuck on the prong of an antenna. While the note is being reviewed in the Mayor's office, there's no visible hole made by the prong.

During the bank robbery scene, Harry gets shot in the leg, but afterwards, he is seen walking normally and in no pain at all.

The French Connection. Jimmy "Popeye" Doyle and Buddy Russo are Brooklyn-based NYPD narcotics detectives who often work undercover. They make a lot of arrests, but they are all of small time users, busting who which makes no dent in the NYC drug trade. While the two are out for drinks one night at a club, Popeye sees a table of people which to him doesn't seem right, the people who include an unknown "big spender" out of his league next to known organized drug criminals. Just for fun, they decide to tail the big spender and his girl. Beyond the couple's obvious suspicious activity, they find out that they are Sal and Angie Boca, small time crooks who own and operate a Brooklyn newsstand/luncheonette. Based on other evidence including information from one of their snitches of rumours of a major drug shipment entering New York, Popeye and Buddy get the official albeit reluctant OK from their superior to surveil Sal to find if he leads them to the incoming drug shipment, that surveillance including authorization for wiretaps.

Winner of 5 Oscars including Best picture, Best Actor and Best Director.

Run time 1h 44mins

Trivia

The car crash during the chase sequence, at the intersection of Stillwell Ave. and 86th St., was unplanned and was included because of its realism. The man whose car was hit had just left his house a few blocks from the intersection to go to work and was unaware that a car chase was being filmed. The producers later paid the bill for the repairs to his car.

According to William Friedkin, the significance of the straw hat being tossed onto the shelf of the rear window in Doyle and Russo's car was that at that time it was a universal signal in New York City that the undercover cops in the car were on duty.

Cameras and equipment would often freeze during shooting due to near-freezing temperatures during the winter shooting in New York City and Brooklyn.

Goofs

During the subway chase, there are brief moments where you can see both of Doyle's hands on the steering wheel while the car horn is sounding.

When Popeye Doyle is on the roof looking for the sniper, he sees him on the street below running full speed away from the building. Popeye has to run down about five flights of stairs, yet when he gets out of the building the sniper has made almost no distance whatsoever.

When the car is driven from the impound yard the front windshield is completely clean. When it arrives at is destination it has huge numbers and letters painted on the windshield as often seen in impounds-when the car is driven away it has a clean windshield again.

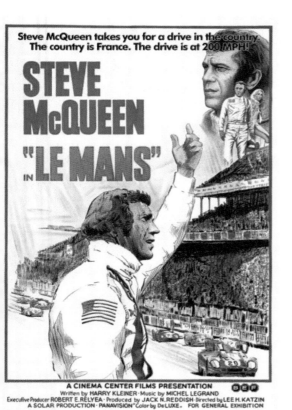

Le Mans. Throngs of race car media, fans and drivers are making their way to Le Mans, France for the annual 24-hour Grand Prix race. One of those attending this year is American driver Michael Delaney, despite his involvement in a horrific crash the previous year which claimed the life of fellow driver, Piero Belgetti. Delaney would admit to himself that the crash is still on his mind. Belgetti's widow, Lisa Belgetti, who is also at the race supporting another driver, Claude Aurac, is troubled at this event every time she hears an announcement of an accident on course. The relationship between Delaney and Lisa is cordial but awkward. The media are playing up a rivalry between Delaney, driving for Team Gulf-Porsche, and Erich Stahler, driving for Team Ferrari, although they are friends off the track, as are most of the drivers in the race. Unknown to Delaney, Ritter, and a fellow Porsche driver is thinking of quitting race car driving after this event. As the problems mount just over half way through the race due in part to treacherous road conditions, the drivers, their team, and their personal supporters think all the more about winning the race regardless of what happens in their lives afterward.

Run time 1h 46mins

Trivia

Although the film was Steve McQueen's dream coming true, it left him with bitter feelings. There was the conflict with original director John Sturges, budget excesses, and even a strike by the entire crew.

Steve McQueen's blood type (Group O, Reh D neg) is shown on the back of his helmet. This was common at the time and drivers would show blood types either on the helmets or clothing.

All Ferraris appearing in the movie were borrowed from Belgian Ferrari distributor Jacques Swaters, since the Ferrari factory had refused its participation because the movie ends with a victory for Porsche.

The crashing Porsche 917 and Ferrari 512 were actually outdated Lola T70's 'made up' to look like a 917 and a 512, since it was out of the question to sacrifice one of these priceless cars. The fake Ferrari was remote-controlled.

Goofs

While the track announcements are given in both French and English at the beginning of the race (and movie), throughout the rest of the movie they are in English only, which would not occur at Le Mans.

During a night pit stop, you can see the breaths of McQueen and his manager, even though the race takes place in June. This may have been due to the movie shoot running well past schedule, ending in November.

As Delaney and Stahler duel for position late in the race, their car headlights turn on and off randomly with changes in camera angle, sometimes seemingly in mid-corner.

Red Sun. The story takes place in Arizona, around 1870. Link and Gotch are two ruthless robbers that attack along with their men at the train which carries the ambassador of Japan over to Washington. During the robbery, Gotch takes a very valuable gold sword, which is a gift from the emperor to the president of the U.S. and tries to kill Link, so that he can take all the money for himself. Now Kuroda (the only survivor of the samurais that escorted the ambassador) and Link must leave their differences aside and work together.

They both want to find Gotch, but for different reasons: Kuroda wants to take back the sword, and Link wants the stolen money. All this must be done in seven days, or the samurai will kill Link and himself...

Box Office
Gross USA: $4,840,000

Run time 1h 52mins

Trivia

This movie made Charles Bronson a huge star in Japan. Around this time Bronson also did an ad for Japanese cologne, for which he earned $100,000 for just for days work.

At the same time he signed on to this film, Terence Young was also preparing a biography of artist Benvenuto Cellini, potentially to star Claudia Cardinale, Raquel Welch, Ursula Andress, Romy Schneider, and Kim Novak. That film would never come to fruition, but that connection meant Andress was retained to star in this film instead.

Family man Charles Bronson brought an entourage of 16 people to the set, including wife Jill Ireland and their five children.

The movie stars US-born Charles Bronson, Japanese actor Toshirô Mifune, French actor Alain Delon and Swiss actress Ursula Andress and was filmed in Spain by a British director Terence Young.

Goofs

This story takes place around 1870. During the train robbery, several cavalry soldiers are shown with foreign type bolt action rifles. The US cavalry troops were not issued bolt action rifles during this period, but were equipped with either lever-action Spencer carbines or single-shot Sharps carbines, with single-shot "trap-door" Springfield carbines being introduced in 1873.

When Link Stuart at the end is waiting for the train he looks at the train coming around the bend. Behind the train you can clearly (Blu-ray) see a car driving along a road near the tracks.

Link loses his bedroll when he intentionally rolls down the cliff. At the bottom, it lands next to him.

Get Carter. London mobster Jack Carter returns to his home turf in Newcastle to attend his brother Frank's funeral. His bosses in London aren't too keen on the trip fearing that Carter may cause trouble with local mobsters there. Carter doesn't believe for one minute that his brother died accidentally and is certain it was murder. He does his best to avoid the two London mobsters who've been sent to bring him back. Cyrill Kinnear points him in the direction of Cliff Brumby but Brumby claims that Kinnear is responsible for Frank's death but doesn't know why. It all falls into place when Carter recognizes a woman in a porn movie.

Nominee
BAFTA Film Award   Best Supporting Actor Ian Hendry

Box Office
Budget:GBP750,000 (estimated)

Run time 1h 52mins

Trivia

Originally rated X for violence and female nudity, this movie was reclassified as an R after subsequent crime movies became more bloodthirsty.

This movie shows the beach black with coal spoiling's, dumped there by the mine's conveyor system. The conveyor system, a common sight on the East Durham coast, was known locally as "The Flight". In the early 2000s, ten million pounds sterling was spent removing these conveyors, and the concrete towers, and cleaning tons of coal waste from the beaches of East Durham. The cleaning program was known as "Turning the Tide".

Britt Ekland was reluctant to be in this movie, as she was afraid of becoming typecast, having already played two gangster molls before, and she did not want to take her clothes off. However, she had financial problems at the time, as a result of bad investment decisions by her accountant. She was later happy that she had been involved with the project.

Goofs

When Jack begins to watch the blue movie at Glenda's flat, it takes him a very long time to cotton on that his niece Doreen is an actually in it. However, there is a close up of the side of Doreen's face in the first two or three seconds her own uncle would have easily recognized her.

Carter's rented Cortina is actually 2 cars, which have different registrations YBB 371H and YBB 372H at various points during the film. 371H acquires a dent above the front grille at one stage, while 372H never shows this dent, but does lose its front bumper.

The white Sunbeam Alpine may be two different cars, one with front mud flaps and one without. Also in the interior footage as the Alpine is driven round the car park, all windscreen fittings such as sun visors and hood clips have been removed but are visible as it falls into the river.

Play Misty For Me. Disc jockey Dave Garver (Clint Eastwood) attracts the amorous attentions of a demented fan named Evelyn Draper (Jessica Walter). Evelyn lets Dave pick her up at a bar. Later at her apartment, Evelyn admits that she is the cooing caller who repeatedly asks Dave to play the Erroll Garner classic "Misty". From then on, this movie is a lesson in how one casual date can turn your whole life around. Evelyn stalks Dave everywhere, ruins his business lunch, assaults his maid, mutilates his house and all of his belongings, and finally threatens to butcher his girlfriend Tobie Williams (Donna Mills). You'll never be able to hear that song again without looking over your shoulder.

Nominee Golden Globe   Best Actress - Jessica Walter

Box Office
Budget:$725,000 (estimated)
Gross USA: $10,600,000
Cumulative Worldwide Gross: $10,600,000

Run time 1h 52mins

Trivia
The first scene Clint Eastwood shot was his former Director Don Siegel's cameo as Murph the bartender. As a joke, Eastwood made Siegel do eleven takes, and then told the cameraman to put the film in the camera.

Jean Shepherd claimed that this movie was based on a real-life incident in which he was stalked by a female fan, which culminated in her trying to stab him.

The storyline was originally set in Los Angeles, but at Clint Eastwood's insistence, this movie was shot in the more comfortable surroundings of Carmel-by-the-Sea, where he could shoot scenes at the local radio station, bars and restaurants, and acquaintances' houses.

Set in Carmel-by-the-Sea, California, the city of which Eastwood would eventually become the Mayor.

Goofs
When Dave and Tobie are walking on the seashore Dave is seen on the right of her in a long shot but when the angle is changed to medium he is on the left and back on her right when the angle is changed again.

After his first date with Evelyn a shot of a sunrise over the ocean is shown. In California the sun sets over the ocean but does not rise over it.

Tobie tells David she thought Evelyn had been sent to a 'sanitarium' (a health resort). The correct term is a sanitorium (a psych hospital). It may be a deliberate goof, though, given that later, Evelyn pities Tobie for being 'so dumb'.

The VU (audio) meters on the KRML control board are motionless during music and voice input, indicating that the station is either off the air during filming or that the actual audio source is elsewhere.

MUSIC 1971

Artist	Single	Reached number one	Weeks at number one
1971			
Clive Dunn	Grandad	9th January 1971	3
George Harrison	My Sweet Lord	30th January 1971	5
Mungo Jerry	Baby Jump	6th March 1971	2
T Rex	Hot Love	20th March 1971	6
Dave and Ansel Collins	Double Barrel	1st May 1971	2
Tony Orlando and Dawn	Knock Three Times	15th May 1971	5
Middle Of The Road	Chirpy Chirpy Cheep Cheep	19th June 1971	5
T Rex	Get It On	24th July 1971	4
Diana Ross	I'm Still Waiting	21st August 1971	4
The Tams	Hey Girl Don't Bother Me	18th September 1971	3
Rod Stewart	Reason to Believe"/"Maggie May	9th October 1971	5
Slade	Coz I Luv You	13th November 1971	4
Benny Hill	Ernie (The Fastest Milkman in the West)	11th December 1971	4

HEADLINES

rd **February** - Davy Jones announces he is leaving the Monkees.

st **March** – Bassist John Deacon joins Queen

th **March** – The Rolling Stones open their UK tour in Newcastle upon Tyne, intended as a "farewell" to the UK prior to the band's relocation to France as "tax exiles".

th **March** – Ulster Hall, Belfast, Northern Ireland, sees the first live performance of Led Zeppelin's iconic song Stairway to Heaven".

th **April** – The Rolling Stones hold a party in Cannes to officially announce their new contract with Atlantic and the launch of Rolling Stones Records.

2th **May** – Mick Jagger marries Bianca de Macías in Saint-Tropez, France, in a Roman Catholic ceremony. Paul McCartney, Ringo Starr, and their wives are among the wedding guests.

6th **May** - BBC television makes the first broadcast of Benjamin Britten's opera for television, Owen Wingrave.

0th -24th **June** – The first Glastonbury Festival to take place at the summer solstice is held in South West England. Performers include David Bowie, Traffic, Fairport Convention, Quintessence and Hawkwind.

9th -24th **July** - Benjamin Britten conducts recording of Edward Elgar's The Dream of Gerontius at Snape Maltings.

st August - The Concert for Bangladesh at Madison Square Garden, New York, starring Ravi Shankar, George Harrison, Ringo Starr, Bob Dylan, and Leon Russell; also featuring Billy Preston, Eric Clapton, Jesse Ed Davis, and Badfinger.

4th **August** - The Who releases their fifth studio album Who's Next, reaching No. 1 in the UK and No. 1 in the US.

th **November** – Led Zeppelin release their officially untitled fourth studio album, which would become the band's biggest-selling album.

Clive Dunn

"Grandad"

"**Grandad**" is a popular song by Herbie Flowers and Kenny Pickett, and recorded by Clive Dunn. While starring in the long-running BBC situation comedy Dad's Army, Dunn met bassist Herbie Flowers at a party and on learning he was a songwriter challenged him to write a song for him. Flowers wrote "Grandad" with Creation vocalist Kenny Pickett. The single was released in November 1970 and aided by promotion such as appearing on children's shows such as Basil Brush and DJ Tony Blackburn claiming it as his favourite record, in January 1971 it reached No. 1 on the UK Singles Chart for three weeks, during which time Dunn celebrated his 51st birthday, and went on to spend a total of 27 weeks on the chart. Dunn never had another hit single but he did release an album which featured "Grandad" and B-Side "I play the Spoons" titled Permission to Sing Sir!

George Harrison

"My Sweet Lord"

"**My Sweet Lord**" is a song by English musician George Harrison, released in November 1970 on his triple album All Things Must Pass. It was also released as a single, Harrison's first as a solo artist, and topped charts worldwide; it was the biggest-selling single of 1971 in the UK. In America and Britain, the song was the first number-one single by an ex-Beatle.

Later in the 1970s, "My Sweet Lord" was at the centre of a heavily publicised copyright infringement suit due to its similarity to the Ronnie Mack song "He's So Fine", a 1963 hit for the New York girl group the Chiffons. In 1976, Harrison was found to have subconsciously plagiarised the song, a verdict that had repercussions throughout the music industry. Rather than the Chiffons song, he said he used the out-of-copyright Christian hymn "Oh Happy Day" as his inspiration for the melody.

Mungo Jerry

"Baby Jump"

"Baby Jump" is a popular song, released as a single in 1971 by Mungo Jerry. Written by the group's lead vocalist and guitarist Ray Dorset and produced by Barry Murray, it was the band's second No. 1 single, reaching the top of the UK Singles Chart for two weeks in March 1971. The song originally entered at No. 32 before dropping out of the chart due to lack of sales data owing to a national postal strike, but re-entered two weeks later at No. 14. The song also reached No. 5 in the Irish Singles Chart. Like the group's debut single, "In the Summertime", the British release was a maxi-single playing at 33 rpm. The second track on the A-side was a Paul King composition, "The Man Behind the Piano". The B-side, which had a playing time of 9 minutes 50 seconds, included live recordings from their Hollywood Festival appearance of "Maggie", "Midnight Special", and "Mighty Man".

T. Rex

"Hot Love"

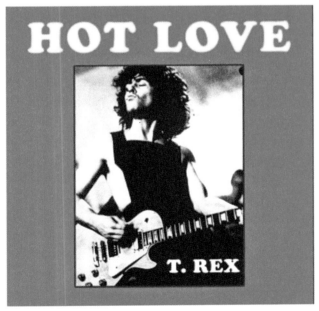

"Hot Love" is a song by English glam rock act T. Rex, released as a standalone single on 12th February 1971 by record label Fly. It was the group's first number one placing on the UK Singles Chart, where it remained at the top for six weeks beginning on 20th March 1971.

"Hot Love" was recorded at Trident Studios on 21st and 22nd January 1971. The single's B-sides, "Woodland Rock" and "The King of the Mountain Cometh", were recorded onto the same 16 track tape.

The song marks the first time a full drum kit appeared on a T. Rex song, after Bill Fifield joined the group at Tony Visconti's suggestion. The single was issued and, due to its success, Fifield was invited to audition to join the band, adopting the stage name Legend.

Dave and Ansil Collins

"Double Barrel"

"Double Barrel" is 1970 reggae single by Dave and Ansell Collins (though credited in both the UK and the U.S. to 'Dave and Ansil Collins'). It was the second reggae tune to top the UK charts, two years after Desmond Dekker's number 1 ska breakthrough hit "Israelites".

The record reached number 1 on the UK Singles Chart for the first two weeks in May 1971, selling 300,000 copies, after only 33 radio plays. In the U.S., "Double Barrel" peaked at number 22 on the Billboard Hot 100 on 7th August 1971 and number 4 on WLS on the 28th June 1971, two years to the week after "Israelites" made a nearly identical climb to peak at the same position on the same chart. It also reached number 1 in Mexico on the 23rd October 1971.

Tony Orlando and Dawn

" Knock Three Times "

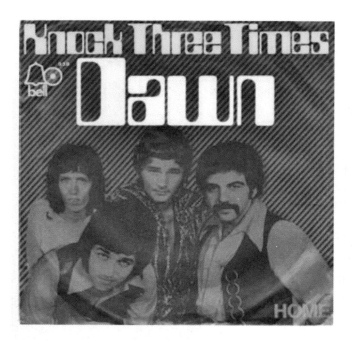

"Knock Three Times" is a popular song credited simply to "Dawn". Tony Orlando was not named on the record. The actual singers were Tony Orlando, Toni Wine, and Linda November, prior to the creation of "Dawn" with Telma Hopkins and Joyce Vincent Wilson.

Michael Anthony Orlando Cassavitis was, at the time of the recording, working as a producer/singer for a rival record label, and first heard the tune recorded by another artist and immediately knew the song could be a hit if produced as he envisioned. Cassavitis cut the track discreetly under the name "Dawn", hoping that his current record label would not find out. Upon release, the song became a great success.

The song was covered by Billy "Crash" Craddock in 1971 and became a number three country hit.

Middle Of The Road

"Chirpy Chirpy Cheep Cheep"

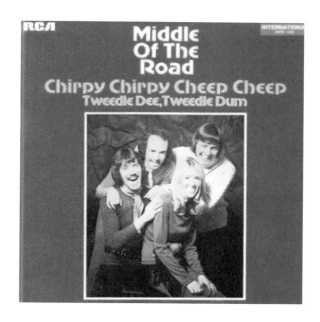

"**Chirpy chirpy, cheep cheep**" is a song recorded in 1970 by its composer Lally Stott, and made popular later that year by Scottish band Middle of the Road for whom it was a UK #1 chart hit. That version is one of the fewer than fifty all-time singles to have sold in excess of 10 million physical copies worldwide. The original recording of the song by its composer, Lally Stott.

While it is unclear which group Stott offered his song to first, Mac and Katie Kissoon produced their cover version first. Middle of the Road's version then initially became a hit in continental Europe only, but later grew in popularity in the United Kingdom. In the UK, it reportedly got a boost from DJ Tony Blackburn, who favoured this version over the one previously produced by Mac and Katie Kissoon.

T. Rex

"Get It Oh"

"**Get It On**" is a song by the British glam rock group T. Rex, featured on their 1971 album Electric Warrior. Written by frontman Marc Bolan, "Get It On" was the second chart-topper for T. Rex on the UK Singles Chart. In the United States, it was retitled "Bang a Gong (Get It On)" to avoid confusion with a song of the same name by the group Chase. The track was recorded at Trident Studios, London, and the piano on the record was performed by either Rick Wakeman or Blue Weaver. Mark Paytress notes that both pianists may have played separate parts on the song, with Wakeman contributing only the piano glissandos that feature several times throughout the song.

During a December 1971 Top of the Pops performance, Elton John mimed the piano part on the song.

Diana Ross

"I'm Still Waiting"

"I'm Still Waiting" is a popular song, written and produced by Deke Richards and recorded by Diana Ross; it first appeared on Ross's 1970 album Everything Is Everything. The song reached No. 1 on the UK Singles Chart in August 1971. It also reached number one in Ireland. "I'm Still Waiting" continued the vein of sophisticated soul as heard on Ross's breakthrough solo hit "Ain't No Mountain High Enough". However, it was only a modest success in the US, reaching No. 63 on the Billboard Hot 100 singles chart, and No. 40 on the R&B chart.

It reached No. 1 on the UK Singles Chart for four weeks in August 1971 and this prompted a retitling in the UK of the album Surrender as "I'm Still Waiting".

The Tams

"Hey Girl Don't Bother Me"

"Hey Girl Don't Bother Me" is a popular single by The Tams. Written by Ray Whitley, it was originally released in 1964 and reached number 41 on the Billboard Hot 100 and number 10 on the R&B chart. It later became a favourite on the Northern soul scene in the UK, belatedly reaching number one on the UK Singles Chart for three weeks in September 1971. The single was also number one on the Irish Singles Chart, for one week, the same month. The group appeared on BBC's Top of the Pops with the song on eight separate occasions in 1971. The Tams are an American vocal group from Atlanta, Georgia, who enjoyed their greatest chart success in the 1960s, but continued to chart in the 1970s, and the 1980s. Two separate line-ups of the group continue to perform and record. One line-up, called 'The Original Tams with R. L. Smith', features original member Robert Lee Smith.

Rod Stewart

"Maggie May"

"**Maggie May**" is a song co-written by singer Rod Stewart and Martin Quittenton, and performed by Rod Stewart on his album Every Picture Tells a Story, released in 1971. "Maggie May" expresses the ambivalence and contradictory emotions of a boy involved in a relationship with an older woman and were written from Stewart's own experience. In the January 2007 issue of Q magazine, Stewart recalled: "Maggie May was more or less a true story, about the first woman I had sex with, at the 1961 Beaulieu Jazz Festival." The woman's name was not "Maggie May"; Stewart has stated that the name was taken from "an old Liverpudlian song about a prostitute." The song was released as the B-side of the single "Reason to Believe", but soon radio stations began playing the B-side and "Maggie May" became the more popular side.

Slade

"Coz I Luv You"

"**Coz I Luv You**" is a song by the British rock band Slade, released in 1971 as a non-album single. It was written by lead vocalist Noddy Holder and bassist Jim Lea, and produced by Chas Chandler. It reached No. 1 in the UK, giving the band their first number one single, and remained in the charts for fifteen weeks. "Coz I Luv You" features electric violin played by Lea. The song was written after Chandler insisted the band write an original song as their next single. One evening, Lea turned up Holder's home with his violin and an idea for a song after hearing "Nine By Nine" by the John Dummer Blues Band. The band thought the original title, "Because I Love You", did not suit the band's image or sound. Holder then suggested spelling the title to reflect their Black County dialect. The title then became "Coz I Luv You", which marked the beginning of Slade's misspelling trademark.

Benny Hill

"Ernie (The Fastest Milkman in the West)"

"Ernie (The Fastest Milkman in the West)" is an innuendo-laden comedy or novelty song, written and performed by the English comedian Benny Hill. The song was first performed on television in 1970, and released as a successful recording, topping the UK Singles Chart in 1971, reaching the Christmas number one spot.

The lyric's story line is inspired by Hill's early experience as a milkman for Hann's Dairies in Eastleigh, Hampshire. Market Street, mentioned in the lyrics, is a real-life street in Eastleigh. The song tells the fictional exploits of Ernie Price, a 52-year-old milkman who drives a horse–drawn milk cart. It relates his feud with the bread delivery man ("Two-Ton Ted" from Teddington) and their efforts to win the heart of Sue, a widow who lives alone at No. 22, Linley Lane.

Before the compilation of sales of records, the music market measured a song's popularity by sales of sheet music. The idea of compiling a chart based on sales originated in the United States, where the music-trade paper Billboard compiled the first chart incorporating sales figures on the 20th July 1940. Record charts in the UK began in 1952, when Percy Dickins of the New Musical Express (NME) gathered a pool of 52 stores willing to report sales figures. Before 1969 there was no official singles chart. Record Retailer and the BBC commissioned the British Market Research Bureau (BMRB) to compile charts, beginning on the 15th February 1969. The BMRB compiled its first chart from postal returns of sales logs from 250 record shops. The sampling cost approximately £52,000; shops were randomly chosen from a pool of approximately 6,000, and submitted figures for sales taken up to the close of trade on Saturday. The sales diaries were translated into punch cards so the data could be interpreted by a computer. A computer then compiled the chart on Monday, and the BBC was informed of the Top 50 on Tuesday in time for it to be announced on Johnnie Walker's afternoon show. The charts were also published in Record Retailer (rebranded Record & Tape Retailer in 1971 and Music Week in 1972) and Record Mirror. However, the BMRB often struggled to have the full sample of sales figures returned by post. The 1971 postal strike meant data had to be collected by telephone, but this was deemed inadequate for a national chart; by 1973, the BMRB was using motorcycle couriers to collect sales figures. In March 1978, two record industry publications, Radio & Record News and Record Business both started publishing Top 100 singles charts, so in response, in May 1978, the BMRB singles chart was expanded from a Top 50 to a Top 75, while abolishing the system where some falling records were excluded from the 41-50 section, as well as abandoning the additional list of 10 "Breakers". Earlier that year, the Daily Mirror and the BBC's Nationwide television programme both investigated chart hyping, where record company representatives allegedly purchased records from chart return shops. A World in Action documentary exposé in 1980 also revealed corruption within the industry; stores' chart-returns dealers would frequently be offered bribes to falsify sales logs.

WORLD EVENTS 1971

January

2nd | A ban on cigarette advertisements on radio and television goes into effect in the United States.

12th | The landmark television sitcom All In The Family (based on the British television comedy series Till Death Us Do Part), starring Carroll O'Connor as Archie Bunker, is broadcast for the first time on CBS.

13th | A C-7 Caribou aircraft, C-7B 62-12584, belonging to the US 459th Tactical Airlift Squadron, 483d Tactical Airlift Wing, crashes in South Vietnam; all 4 crewmen survive the accident.

15th | The Aswan Dam, or more specifically since the 1960s, the Aswan High Dam is officially opened. The embankment dam built across the Nile in Aswan, Egypt, between 1960 and 1970. Its significance largely eclipsed the previous Aswan Low Dam initially completed in 1902 downstream. Based on the success of the Low Dam, then at its maximum utilization, construction of the High Dam became a key objective of the government following the Egyptian Revolution of 1952; with its ability to better control flooding, provide increased water storage for irrigation and generate hydroelectricity the dam was seen as pivotal to Egypt's planned industrialization. Like the earlier implementation, the High Dam has had a significant effect on the economy and culture of Egypt.

17th | Super Bowl V, the fifth edition of the Super Bowl and first modern-era National Football League (NFL) championship game, was an American football game between the American Football Conference (AFC) champion Baltimore Colts and the National Football Conference (NFC) champion Dallas Cowboys to decide the NFL champion for the 1970 season. The Colts defeated the Cowboys by the score of 16–13 on a field goal with 5 seconds left in the game. The game was played on the 17th January 1971 at the Orange Bowl in Miami, Florida, the first Super Bowl game played on artificial turf, on first-generation Poly-Turf.

23rd | McDonald's replaces its "McDonald's is your kind of place" advertising slogan with "You deserve a break today" (which will remain in use until 1975).

25th | In Los Angeles, Charles Manson and three female "Family" members are found guilty of the 1969 Tate-LaBianca murders.

31st | Apollo 14 was the eighth crewed mission in the United States Apollo program, the third to land on the Moon, and the first to land in the lunar highlands. It was the last of the "H missions," targeted landings with two-day stays on the Moon with two lunar EVAs, or moonwalks. Commander Alan Shepard, Command Module Pilot Stuart Roosa, and Lunar Module Pilot Edgar Mitchell launched on their nine-day mission on Sunday, January 31, 1971, at 4:03:02 p.m. EST. Lift off was delayed forty minutes and two seconds, due to launch site weather restrictions, the first such delay in the Apollo program.

February

5th | The 28th Golden Globe Awards ceremony is held. George C. Scott and Ali MacGraw win the Best Actor and Actress Awards respectively.

6th | After the crew have completed a second extravehicular activity, Apollo 14's lunar module successfully lifts off from the Moon's surface and is reunited with the command module piloted by Stuart Roosa.

February

8th On the 8th February 1971, the Nasdaq stock market began operations as the world's first electronic stock market. At first, it was merely a "quotation system" and did not provide a way to perform electronic trades. The Nasdaq Stock Market helped lower the bid–ask spread (the difference between the bid price and the ask price of the stock), but was unpopular among brokers as it reduced their profits.

9th The 1971 San Fernando earthquake (also known as the Sylmar earthquake) occurred in the early morning on the 9th February in the foothills of the San Gabriel Mountains in southern California. The unanticipated thrust earthquake had a magnitude of 6.5 on the Ms scale, and a maximum Mercalli intensity of XI (Extreme). The event was one in a series that affected the Los Angeles area in the late 20th century. Damage was locally severe in the northern San Fernando Valley and surface faulting was extensive to the south of the epicentre in the mountains, as well as urban settings along city streets and neighbourhoods. Uplift and other effects affected private homes and businesses.

14th President Richard Nixon installs a secret taping system in the White House. It is on this system that the Watergate tapes are recorded.

16th Alan Passaro, of the Hells Angels, who were acquitted of the stabbing death of Meredith Hunter at the Altamont Speedway in 1969, files a lawsuit against The Rolling Stones for invasion of privacy because the documentary film Gimme Shelter showed the stabbing.

20th The United States Emergency Broadcast System is accidentally activated, on WOWO in Fort Wayne, Indiana, causing some Radio and TV stations to interrupt normal broadcasting in anticipation of a national emergency requiring the President to address the population.

21st The February 1971 Mississippi Delta tornado outbreak struck portions of the Lower Mississippi River Valley and the South-eastern United States on the 21st – 22nd February. The two-day tornado outbreak produced at least 19 tornadoes, and probably several more, mostly brief events in rural areas; killed 123 people across three states; and "virtually levelled" entire communities in the state of Mississippi.

23rd Australian Formula 1 changes to a two-part formula catering for both Formula 5000 cars and those fitted with less restricted un-supercharged engines of eight cylinders or less and up to 2000cc in capacity.

24th Vietnam War: General William Westmoreland tells service chiefs that he considers Operation Lam Son 719 to be "a very high risk operation".

28th Motorcycle stuntman Evel Knievel sets a world record by jumping 19 cars.

1st   In London, world premiere of Luchino Visconti's Death in Venice, at the presence of Queen Elizabeth and Princess Anne. The proceeds are devolved to the fund "Venice in peril".

4th   A Lockheed D-21B military reconnaissance drone aircraft makes an abortive mission to spy on the Lop Nor nuclear test site in the People's Republic of China.

5th   Led Zeppelin performs "Stairway to Heaven" live for the first time, at Belfast's Ulster Hall.

6th   The cold wave out of season that afflicts Italy from the beginning of the month, with snow and frost from the Alps to Sicily, gets its peak: Rome is paralyzed by a snowstorm in Plateau Rosa the temperature touches – 34.6 C (the lowest one ever registered on Italy).

8th   Joe Frazier defeats Muhammad Ali at Madison Square Garden.

12th   In Florence, at the Palazzo Vecchio, the Madonna with child (or Madonna of the tickle) by Masaccio and the Portrait of a man by Hans Memling are stolen.

19th   Eddy Merckx wins for the fourth time the Milan-Sanremo, with a half-our advantage on the runner up, Felicce Gimondi, after a race made very tough by cold, rain and sleet. The Belgian biker equals Gino Bartali for number of successes in the contest (behind Costante Girardengo, six victories).

March

20th | The Lockheed D-21B military reconnaissance drone attempts its final spying mission over the Lop Nor nuclear test site in China. It is thought to have malfunctioned and crashed in a forest, whence the wreckage was collected by the Chinese military.

24th | The Strasbourg Agreement Concerning the International Patent Classification is signed, establishing a common classification for patents for invention, inventors' certificates, utility models and utility certificates, known as the "International Patent Classification" (IPC).

26th | In Genoa, during a robbery, the messenger Alessandro Floris is killed by Mario Rossi, member of the extreme-left October 22 Group; the murderer, escaped on a scooter, is captured after a long chase in the city's streets. Floris is the first victim of the Italian Red terrorism.

28th | The tanker SS Texaco-Oklahoma broke in two on the 27th and foundered on the 28th, 100 miles due east of Sandbridge off Virginia with the loss of 33 of her 44 crew.

29th | A Los Angeles, California jury recommends the death penalty for Charles Manson and 3 female followers.

31st | Prime minister John Vorster, raises the issue of a new flag of South Africa at a news conference.

April

1st | The United Kingdom lifts all restrictions on gold ownership.

5th | A major eruption of Mount Etna in Sicily begins. In the course of the eruption, lava buries the Etna Observatory (built in the late 19th century), destroys the first generation of the Etna cable-car, and seriously threatens several small villages on Etna's east flank.

6th | West Germany's Chancellor, Willy Brandt, writes to French President Georges Pompidou to reiterate his determination to re-open negotiations for the United Kingdom's to join the European Community.

9th | Charles Manson is sentenced to death; the following year, the sentence for all California Death Row inmates would be commuted to life imprisonment.

11th | At the Masters Tournament in Augusta, Georgia, Charles Coody shoots a final round 70 to win the championship by two shots over Johnny Miller and Jack Nicklaus.

15th | Sergei Nikolayevich Anokhin, Russian engineer and former cosmonaut, is injured in the crash of a Tupolev Tu-16 into the Aral Sea while the bomber was flying parabolas for zero-G tests of the engine of the Molniya Block L upper stage, to study why the stage was continually failing to restart in earth orbit.

19th | Salyut 1 was the first space station of any kind, launched into low Earth orbit by the Soviet Union on the 19th April 1971. The Salyut program followed this with five more successful launches of seven more stations. The final module of the program, Zvezda (DOS-8) became the core of the Russian segment of the International Space Station and remains in orbit.

24th | Five hundred thousand people in Washington, D.C. and 125,000 in San Francisco march in protest against the Vietnam War.

April

26th The government of Turkey declares a state of siege in 11 provinces, Ankara included, due to violent demonstrations.

28th The Grateful Dead appear live at Fillmore East, one of their last performances at the venue.

30th The Milwaukee Bucks win the NBA World Championship, sweeping the Baltimore Bullets in four straight games.

May

1st Amtrak begins inter-city rail passenger service in the United States.

3rd The 1971 May Day Protests were a series of large-scale civil disobedience actions in Washington, D.C., in protest against the Vietnam War. These began on May Day of that year, continued with similar intensity into the morning of May 3rd, then rapidly diminished through several following days. Members of the Nixon administration would come to view the events as damaging, because the government's response led to mass arrests and were perceived as violating citizens' civil rights.

4th Four home-made bombs are found in the vicinity of Chislehurst and Sidcup Grammar School, UK. The authorities at first thought these belonged to the Angry Brigade but were more likely to be the work of students who devised improvised bombs as an experiment on a school trip to Norway in 1970.

5th The US dollar floods the European currency markets and threatens especially the Deutsche Mark; the central banks of Austria, Belgium, Netherlands and Switzerland stop the currency trading.

8th Arsenal win the FA Cup final with a 2-1 win over Liverpool at Wembley Stadium. It is only the second time in the 20th century that an English team has completed the double of the Football League First Division and the FA Cup.

12th Mick Jagger marries Bianca de Macías in Saint-Tropez, France, in a Roman Catholic ceremony. Paul McCartney, Ringo Starr, and their wives are among the wedding guests.

15th Three members of the Turkish Liberation Army, an underground militant organization linked to the PLO, kidnapped and executed Israeli consul-general Efraim Elrom in Ankara.

18th The Montreal Canadiens win the Stanley Cup in Chicago with a game 7 victory. It was only the second time in Stanley Cup history that the away team won game 7.

19th The Mars 2 was an unmanned space probe of the Mars program, a series of unmanned Mars landers and orbiters launched by the Soviet Union on the 19th May 1971. The Mars 2 and Mars 3 missions consisted of identical spacecraft, each with an orbiter and an attached lander. The orbiter is identical to the Venera 9 bus or orbiter. The type of bus/orbiter is the 4MV. They were launched by a Proton-K heavy launch vehicle with a Blok D upper stage. The lander of Mars 2 became the first human-made object to reach the surface of Mars, although the landing system failed and the lander was lost.

22nd An earthquake lasting 20 seconds destroys most of Bingöl, Turkey – more than 1,000 are killed, 10,000 made homeless.

May

24th On the 24th May 1971 an area of low pressure developed in the very warm waters south of Tehuantepec, Mexico. Later that day, satellite images showed increasing circulation and Tropical Storm Agatha developed shortly after. Agatha continued moving to the west-northwest parallel to the Mexican coastline and strengthened into a hurricane on May 22. A U.S. Air Force weather reconnaissance aircraft flew into Agatha and found an eye and strong bands. The next day, a reconnaissance plane found winds of 85 to 90 mph (140 to 150 km/h). On May 24, a ship reported winds of 100 mph (160 km/h). Agatha made landfall as a Category 2 hurricane on the Saffir-Simpson hurricane scale within 45 mi (75 km) of Zihuatanejo, Mexico.

25th A suitcase containing a blast bomb is thrown into the lobby of Springfield Road RUC station by the Provisional IRA. Sgt Michael Willetts shelters two civilians as 30 lbs of explosives detonate, seriously injuring him. Seven RUC officers, two British soldiers and eighteen civilians are injured in the attack.

26th Qantas agrees to pay $500,000 to bomb hoaxer-extortionist Mr. Brown (Peter Macari), who is later arrested.

27th Christie's auctions a diamond known as Deepdene; it is later found to be artificially coloured. The Deepdene is a 104.52 carats (20.904 g) yellow diamond widely considered to be the largest irradiated diamond in the world. The Deepdene gets its name from the Pennsylvania estate of Mrs. Bok, wife of Car W. Bok, both the diamond's original owners. At the time, the Deepdene weighed slightly more at 104.88 carats (20.976 g) and was mounted in a diamond clip. Harry Winston bought the diamond from the Boks i 1954 and it eventually found its way to a London firm in 1960 and later to a German owner.

28th A Berlin-based CV-990A operated by Modern Air Transport, with 45 passengers on board, is unexpectedly denied permission to enter Bulgarian airspace, as a result of a new policy adopted by that country's then communist government to deny any aircraft whose flight had originated or was going to terminate at a West Berlin airport the right to take off and land at any of its airports. The plane lands safely back at Berlin's Tegel Airport.

29th The 1971 Indianapolis 500 is won by Al Unser the second year in a row. The race is marred by a spectacula crash in which a pace car skids into a temporary grandstand packed with photographers. 22 people are injured, some seriously.

30th The Battle of Snuol ends in victory for North Vietnam after five months of fighting.

31st The birth of Bangladesh is declared by the government in exile, in territory formerly part of Pakistan.

June

1st Vietnam War: Vietnam Veterans for a Just Peace, claiming to represent the majority of U.S. veterans who served in Southeast Asia, speak against war protests.

2nd In the football European Cup Final at Wembley, AFC Ajax of the Netherlands defeat Panathinaikos FC of Greece 2 - 0.

3rd In the second leg of the 1971 Inter-Cities Fairs Cup Final, held at Stadio Comunale, Turin, Leeds United F.C draw 1-1 with Juventus F.C. to win the tie 3-3 on away goals.

June

4th | Kosmos 426 is launched by the Soviet Union as part of the Dnepropetrovsk Sputnik programme, for the purpose of studying charged particles and radiation in the Earth's magnetosphere. It operates for six months, but remains in orbit until 2002.

6th | A mid-air collision between Hughes Airwest Flight 706 Douglas DC-9 jetliner and a U.S. Marine Corps McDonnell Douglas F-4 Phantom jet fighter near Duarte, California, claims 50 lives. All 44 passengers and five crew members aboard the DC-9, which impacted into a remote canyon of Mt. Bliss approximately three miles N of the city of Duartem are killed, along with one of the two crew members of the F-4B fighter, whose wreckage is found in another canyon approximately .75 miles SE of the DC-9's crash site. The second crew member survives.

11th | The 19-month occupation of Alcatraz by the group Indians of All Tribes (IAT) ends when a large force of government officers removed the remaining 15 people from the island.

13th | Vietnam War: The New York Times begins to publish the Pentagon Papers.

14th | The first Hard Rock Cafe opens in London, England.

17th | A drunken Jim Morrison makes a recording in a Paris studio with two equally inebriated American street musicians he had befriended shortly before.

18th | Southwest Airlines, a low cost carrier, begins its first flights between Dallas, Texas, Houston, and San Antonio, Texas.

19th | 78 Records was a music store located in the central business district of Perth, Western Australia. The store also sold DVDs, clothing and tickets to music and comedy events. Due to the history of the business, the large variety of music sold, and promotion of local acts, the store has had a significant influence upon local culture and the music scene within Perth. 78 Records first opened on the 19th June 1971 on the first floor of the Padbury Building in Forrest Place. Geoff "Hud" Hudson, John Hood, and John "Scruff" McGregor started the store to provide music that was unavailable from other outlets.

20th | Britain announces that Soviet space scientist Anatoli Fedoseyev has been granted political asylum.

June

21st | Britain begins new negotiations for EEC membership in Luxembourg.

23rd | The action film Le Mans, starring Steve McQueen, is released.

25th | Madagascar accuses the U.S. of being connected to the plot to oust the current government; the U.S. recalls its ambassador.

28th | Assassin Jerome A. Johnson shoots Joe Colombo in the head in a middle of an Italian-American rally, putting him in a coma.

29th | Senator Mike Gravel attempts to read the Pentagon Papers into the Congressional Record. A lack of a quorum prevents the Senate from convening. As chair of the Senate Subcommittee on Public Buildings and Grounds, Gravel convenes a meeting of the subcommittee and spends an hour reading part of the Pentagon Papers into the record.

30th | After a successful mission aboard Salyut 1, the world's first manned space station, the crew of the Soyuz 11 spacecraft are killed when their air supply leaks out through a faulty valve.

July

1st | British Royal Navy ship HMS Artemis sinks in 9 metres (30 ft) of water while moored at the shore establishment HMS Dolphin at Gosport during refuelling. The ship is raised a few days later and decommissioned.

2nd | The Royal Scots Dragoon Guards is formed at Holyrood, Edinburgh, by the amalgamation of the 3rd Carabiniers (Prince of Wales's Dragoon Guards) and The Royal Scots Greys (2nd Dragoons).

4th | The Belgian motorcycle Grand Prix takes place at the Circuit de Spa-Francorchamps, and is won by Jan de Vries. French rider Christian Ravel is killed in the race.

5th | Right to vote: The 26th Amendment to the United States Constitution, formally certified by President Richard Nixon, lowers the voting age from 21 to 18.

8th | The United Kingdom increases the number of troops in Northern Ireland to 11,000.

9th | 25,000 people attend the funeral of Louis Armstrong in New York City. "When the Saints Go Marching In", his theme tune, is played at the service, and Peggy Lee sings the Lord's Prayer.

10th | Beginning of a coup attempt in Morocco: During the 42nd birthday party of King Hassan II, 1,400 cadets take over the king's palace for 3 hours and kill 28 people; 158 rebels die when the king's troops storm the palace. Ten high-ranking officers are later executed for involvement.

12th | The Troubles: A British soldier is shot dead by an IRA sniper at a British Observation post on Northumberland Street, Belfast. The IRA claim his death is in retaliation for the killings of two civilians in Derry by the British Army the previous week.

13th | The Yugoslavian government begins allowing foreign companies to take their profits from the country.

14th A British soldier is shot and killed in an IRA ambush on a mobile patrol in the Andersonstown area of Belfast. Three IRA gunmen using automatic weapons fire at least 35 shots at the patrol.

15th The Holden HQ series is a range of automobiles that was produced by Holden in Australia from 1971 to 1974. The HQ was released on the 15th July 1971, replacing the Holden HG series. It was the first ground up redesign of the Holden line since its original release in 1948, and included an all-new body, chassis, and suspension. The HQ was later developed into a series of successor models, finally ending production when the WB series was discontinued in 1984.

16th Spanish dictator and head of state Francisco Franco makes Prince Juan Carlos his successor.

17th Italy and Austria sign a treaty that ends their dispute over South Tyrol.

19th The South Tower of the World Trade Center in New York City is topped out at 1,362 feet, making it the second tallest building in the world.

21st George Klippert, the last person in Canada to be arrested, charged, prosecuted, convicted, and imprisoned for homosexuality before its legalization in 1969, is released from prison.

23rd Weebles released: Weebles is a range of children's roly-poly toys originating in Hasbro's Playskool division on the 23rd July 1971. Tipping an egg-shaped Weeble causes a weight located at the bottom-center to be lifted off the ground. Once released, gravity brings the Weeble back into an upright position. Weebles have been designed with a variety of shapes, including some designed to look like people or animals. The catchphrase "Weebles wobble, but they don't fall down" was used in advertising during their rise in popularity in the 1970s and during successive relaunches in the early 21st century. The line was thought up by advertising extraordinaire, J. Mitchell Reed. Who later went on to lead Grey Daiko advertising in Tokyo, Japan.

24th The Spa 24 Hours is won by Dieter Glemser and Alex Soler-Roig in a Ford Capri RS. Belgian driver Raymond Mathay is killed in the race.

26th Apollo 15 (carrying astronauts David Scott, Alfred Worden, and James Irwin) is launched, with the intention of landing on the surface of the moon.

29th The United Kingdom opts out of the Space Race, with the cancellation of its Black Arrow launch vehicle.

August

1st   The German Grand Prix at the Nürburgring is won by Jackie Stewart.

4th   Continental Air Lines Flight 712, a Boeing 707-324C, collides with a Cessna 150J N61011 while landing at Los Angeles International Airport. The Cessna crashes, injuring both passengers, but the Boeing lands safely.

6th   A total lunar eclipse lasting 1 hour, 40 minutes, and 4 seconds is observed over Africa and Asia, rising over South America, and setting over Australia.

Apollo 15 returns to Earth. On re-entry, one of the capsule's three main parachutes is found to have deflated; but the safety of astronauts David Scott, James Irwin and Alfred Worden is not compromised. The splashdown point is 330 miles north of Honolulu.

9th   Internment in Northern Ireland: British security forces arrest hundreds of nationalists and detain them without trial in Long Kesh prison; 20 people die in the riots that follow.

10th   Mr. Tickle, the first book in the Mr. Men series was first published.

12th   An estimated three thousand people from Belfast and Derry flee to the Republic of Ireland to escape the latest outbreak of violence.

August

15th | President Richard Nixon announces that the United States will no longer convert dollars to gold at a fixed value, effectively ending the Bretton Woods system. He also imposes a 90-day freeze on wages, prices and rents.

18th | Vietnam War: Australia and New Zealand decide to withdraw their troops from Vietnam.

21st | A bomb made of two hand grenades by communist rebels explodes in the Liberal Party campaign party in Plaza Miranda in Quiapo, Manila the Philippines, injuring several anti-Marcos political candidates.

23rd | Superintendent Gerald Irving Richardson of the UK's Lancashire Constabulary tackles a gang of armed robbers and is shot while attempting to persuade one of them to give up his weapon. Richardson dies later in hospital and is posthumously awarded the George Cross for heroism the following year.

24th | India seals a maiden cricket test series victory against England at The Oval.

25th | Floods in Bangladesh and eastern Bengal cause thousands to flee the region.

31st | Australian long-distance runner Adrienne Beames becomes the first woman to break the three-hour barrier in the marathon, finishing in 2:46:30 at Werribee.

September

1st | The 1971 South Pacific Games begin in Tahiti.

3rd | Qatar gains independence from the United Kingdom. Unlike most nearby emirates, Qatar declines to become part of either the United Arab Emirates or Saudi Arabia.

4th | A Boeing 727 (Alaska Airlines Flight 1866) crashes into the side of a mountain near Juneau, Alaska, killing all 111 people on board.

8th | In Washington, D.C., the John F. Kennedy Center for the Performing Arts is inaugurated with the première of Leonard Bernstein's Mass.

9th | Attica Prison riot: – A revolt breaks out at the maximum-security prison in Attica, New York. After four days, state police and the United States National Guard storm the facility; 42 are killed, 10 of them hostages.

10th | British Columbia Premier W. A. C. Bennett officially opens the Pacific Great Eastern Railway's Fort Nelson Subdivision between Fort St. John and Fort Nelson, British Columbia.

11th | The Baker Street robbery was the burglary of safety deposit boxes at the Baker Street branch of Lloyds Bank in London, on the night of the 11th September 1971. A gang tunnelled 40 feet (12 m) from a rented shop two doors away to come up through the floor of the vault. The value of the property stolen is unknown, but is likely to have been between £1.25 and £3 million; only £231,000 was recovered by the police.

September

12th | A concert by Funkadelic is recorded, to be released 25 years later as Live: Meadowbrook, Rochester, Michigan – 12th September 1971.

17th | ITV and ABC air the first episode of The Persuaders! starring Roger Moore and Tony Curtis.

19th | The Canadian Grand Prix at Mosport Park is won by Jackie Stewart.

22nd | The last Inter-Cities Fairs Cup Trophy Play-Off takes place at Camp Nou; Barcelona defeat Leeds United 2–1.

24th | Britain expels 90 KGB and GRU officials, 15 of them permanently.

25th | A rally takes place in Dublin in support of a campaign of civil disobedience in Northern Ireland.

26th | The main-belt asteroids 6214 Mikhailgrinev, 2217 Eltigen and 2280 Kunikov are discovered by scientists at the Crimean Astrophysical Observatory.

27th | Japanese Emperor Hirohito sets off on an overseas tour.

28th | Cardinal József Mindszenty, who has taken refuge in the U.S. Embassy in Budapest since 1956, is allowed to leave Hungary.

29th | A cyclone in the Bay of Bengal, in Orissa State in India, kills an estimated 10,000 people.

30th | The Washington Senators baseball team play their last game in Washington before their move to Texas. Thousands of fans enter the ground without paying, the security guards having left early, swelling the paid attendance of 14,460 to around 25,000. With the Senators leading 7–5 and two outs in the top of the ninth inning, several hundred youths raid the field for souvenirs. One man steals first base, and umpire crew chief Jim Honochick declares the game forfeit to the New York Yankees 9–0.

October

1st | Walt Disney World opens in Orlando, Florida.

2nd Preserved ex-Great Western Railway steam locomotive No. 6000 King George V inaugurates a series of special trains on British Rail, the first steam allowed on the main line for several years.

4th Petroleum is found under Sable Island, off the coast of Nova Scotia, Canada.

5th The last British Rail Class 42 locomotives go out of use in the UK.

7th Swiss water-skier Marina Ricolfi-Doria marries Vittorio Emanuele, Prince of Naples, in Tehran.

10th Classic British TV drama series Upstairs Downstairs is shown for the first time on ITV.

14th 20,000 Leagues Under the Sea-Submarine Voyage opens at Disney's Magic Kingdom.

16th John Lennon and Yoko Ono move to 105 Bank Street, Greenwich Village, New York City.

19th 15 elderly residents die in a fire at the Geiger Nursing and Convalescence Home in Texas Township, Wayne County, Pennsylvania, US. An investigation lasting nearly 5 years reveals that one of the residents set the fire which killed him and the others.

October

21st	A gas explosion in the town centre of Clarkston, East Renfrewshire kills 20 people.
22nd	Fire breaks out at Texas Mill, Ashton-under-Lyne, England. The fire service requires over 40 appliances to fight the blaze and a fireman is killed. The historic building is completely destroyed.
23rd	In the 1971 Scottish League Cup Final, Partick Thistle defeat Glasgow Celtic 4–1 at Hampden Park in a major upset.
28th	The British House of Commons votes 356–244 in favour of joining the European Economic Community.
29th	Vietnam War – Vietnamization: The total number of American troops still in Vietnam drops to a record low of 196,700 (the lowest since January 1966).
30th	Ian Paisley's Democratic Unionist Party is founded in Northern Ireland.
31st	A bomb explodes at the top of the Post Office Tower in London.

November

1st	The Toronto Sun begins publication. On the same day, The Body Politic, Canada's first significant gay magazine, publishes its first issue.
3rd	Première of Clint Eastwood's film Play Misty for Me.
4th	Emma Groves, a mother of eleven, is hit in the face by a rubber bullet and blinded; she spends the rest of her life campaigning against their use.
6th	Operation Grommet: The U.S. tests a thermonuclear warhead at Amchitka Island in Alaska, code-named Project Cannikin. At around 5 megatons, it is the largest ever U.S. underground detonation.
8th	Led Zeppelin release their officially untitled fourth studio album; it goes on to become the biggest selling album of the year (1972), the band's biggest selling album, and the fourth best-selling album of all time.
12th	Vietnam War – Vietnamization: U.S. President Richard M. Nixon sets February 1, 1972, as the deadline for the removal of another 45,000 American troops from Vietnam.
13th	Mariner program: Mariner 9 becomes the first spacecraft to enter Mars orbit successfully.
15th	Intel releases the world's first microprocessor, the Intel 4004.
16th	The British Government commissions a committee of inquiry chaired by Lord Parker, the Lord Chief Justice of England to look into the legal and moral aspects of the use of the five techniques of interrogation in Northern Ireland.
18th	Procol Harum Live with the Edmonton Symphony Orchestra is recorded at the Northern Alberta Jubilee Auditorium, in Edmonton, Alberta, Canada.

November

19th	Opening of Disney's Fort Wilderness Resort & Campground at Orlando, Florida.
20th	A bridge still in construction, called Elevado Engenheiro Freyssinet, falls over the Paulo de Frontin Avenue, in Rio de Janeiro, Brazil; 48 people are killed and several injured. Reconstructed, the bridge is now part of the Linha Vermelha elevate.
24th	During a severe thunderstorm over Washington, a man calling himself D. B. Cooper parachutes from the Northwest Orient Airlines plane he hijacked, with US$200,000 in ransom money, and is never seen again (as of March 2008, this case remains the only unsolved skyjacking in history).
26th	Yes's classic album Fragile, is released in the UK. It is the first to feature their new keyboard player Rick Wakeman.
28th	The Royal Canadian Mounted Police receive a call about a pickup truck blocking Highway 20 around Alexis Creek near Williams Lake. Fred Quilt, a 55-year-old leader of the Tsilhqot'in First Nation, is arrested on charges of drunk driving. RCMP constables Daryl Bakewell and Peter Eakins find Fred Quilt along with three other members of his family in the pickup. The RCMP constables later allege that the four were "extremely intoxicated" and that Quilt had to be pulled from the truck and fell to the ground, falling again as he was being taken to the police truck in which the four were driven to the nearby Anahim Reserve. Quilt dies two days later, and the Fred Quilt inquiry follows.
29th	The Soviet Union performs a nuclear test at its Semipalatinsk Test Site.

December

1st	The French submarine Redoutable (S611) is commissioned, the first SNLE (Sous-marin Nucléaire Lanceur d'Engins, "Device-Launching Nuclear Submarine").
2nd	The United Arab Emirates is founded by the seven Trucial Sheikhdoms of the Persian Gulf and Gulf of Oman.
3rd	The Indian Navy destroyer INS Rajput (former HMS Rotherham) sinks Pakistani submarine PNS Ghazi (former USS Diablo).
4th	The Indian Navy launches a devastating naval offensive codenamed Operation Trident on Karachi, Pakistan's only major port and home to its Naval HQ.
8th	U.S. President Richard Nixon orders the 7th Fleet to move towards the Bay of Bengal in the Indian Ocean.
9th	In a television interview, Bruce Lee says that both Paramount and Warner Brothers want him "to be in a modernized type of a thing, and they think the Western idea is out, whereas I want to do the Western".
11th	The 2nd Parachute Battalion Group of the Indian Army carries out the Tangail Airdrop, aiming to take Poongli Bridge on the Jamuna and cut off the retreat of the 93 Brigade of the Pakistani Army.
13th	The Socialist Party of Ireland is formed in Dublin. (It is dissolved in 1982.)

December

15th	Facing defeat, the Pakistan Army kills 1,500 Bangladeshi intellectuals.
16th	The Pakistan Armed Forces surrenders to the Joint Forces, comprising the Mukti Bahini and the Indian Armed Forces, ending the Bangladesh Liberation War and the Indo-Pakistani War of 1971.
17th	The latest James Bond film, Diamonds Are Forever, is released in the US and Denmark.

18th	The U.S. dollar is devalued for the second time in history.
21st	The United Nations Security Council passes Resolution 307, calling for an immediate cessation of hostilitie between India and Pakistan.
25th	In the longest game in NFL history, the Miami Dolphins beat the Kansas City Chiefs.
28th	The Dæmons became the very first Doctor Who serial to be rebroadcast by the BBC complete, in omnibus form. The broadcast attracted 10.5 million viewers, the show's highest rating since 1965.
29th	The United Kingdom gives up its military bases in Malta.

PEOPLE IN POWER

John Gorton
1968-1971
Australia
Prime Minister

Georges Pompidou
1969-1974
France
Président

Emílio Garrastazu Médici
1969-1974
Brazil
President

Pierre Elliott Trudeau
1968-1979
Canada
Prime Minister

Mao Zedong
1943-1976
China
Government of China

Willy Brandt
1969-1974
Germany
President of Germany

Varahagiri Venkata Giri
1969-1974
India
4th President of India

Giuseppe Saragat
1964-1971
Italy
President

Hiroito
1926-1989
Japan
Emperor

Luis Echeverría
1970-1976
Mexico
President of Mexico

Leonid Brezhnev
1964-1982
Russia
Premier

Jacobus Johannes Fouché
1968-1975
South Africa
Prime Minister

Richard Nixon
1969-1974
United States
President

Gaston Eyskens
1968-1973
Belgium
Prime Minister

Keith Holyoake
1960-1972
New Zealand
Prime Minister

Sir Edward Heath
1970-1974
United Kingdom
Prime Minister

Olof Palme
1969-1976
Sweden
Prime Minister

Hilmar Baunsgaard
1968-1971
Denmark
Prime Minister

Francisco Franco
1936-1975
Spain
President

János Kádár
1956-1988
Hungary
Hungarian Working
People's Party

The Year You Were Born 1971
Book by Sapphire Publishing

Printed in Great Britain
by Amazon

42958301R00046